Contents

A HANDBOOK OF TECHNIQUES AND STRATEGIES FOR COACHING STUDENT TEACHERS

Second Edition

Carol Marra Pelletier
Boston College

Allyn and Bacon
Boston   London   Toronto   Sydney   Tokyo   Singapore

To all of the cooperating teachers who
have generously shared their classrooms
with student teachers

Executive editor: Stephen D. Dragin
Series editorial assistant: Bridget McSweeney
Marketing manager: Stephen Smith
Manufacturing buyer: David Repetto

Copyright © 2000, 1995 by Allyn & Bacon
A Pearson Education Company
Needham Heights, MA 02494

Internet: www.abacon.com

Library of Congress Cataloging-in-Publication Data

Pelletier, Carol Marra.
    A handbook of techniques and strategies for coaching student
teachers / Carol Marra Pelletier. -- 2nd ed.
        p.   cm.
    Includes bibliographical references (p.   ).
    ISBN 0-205-30361-7
    1. Student teachers--Training of--United States Handbooks,
manuals, etc.   I. Title.
LB2157.U5P38   1999
370'.71--dc21   99-36246
                                                   CIP

Printed in the United States of America
10 9 8 7 6 5 4 3 2   03 02 01 00

SECTION III   CULMINATING THE STUDENT TEACHING EXPERIENCE   237

Chapter 14   Other Important Issues   239

Chapter 15   Final Evaluation Procedures   255

Acknowledgments

The idea for this handbook started more than 20 years ago when I participated as a cooperating teacher with my first student teacher. This book is the result of my own personal inquiry as a cooperating teacher and of conversations with hundreds of teachers. Many thanks are due to the educators who guided me through this process. In addition, I have been honored to have been the recipient of several grants that have facilitated this work.

The original handbook, titled "So You're Going to Be a Cooperating Practitioner: A Helpful Hints Handbook," was funded by a Horace Mann Grant through the Massachusetts Department of Education. I thank the Department of Education and my local school district in Middleboro, Massachusetts, for funding two grants. One supported the design of the original handbook and the other funded a support program for cooperating teachers who used the book as a basis for collegial conversation. The program was titled *Bridging the Gap: An Empowerment Program for Teacher Preparation*.

A statewide competitive grant called the Lucretia Crocker Fellowship sponsored by the Massachusetts Department of Education allowed me to share the original handbook and the *Bridging the Gap* program across the state of Massachusetts. My Lucretia Crocker colleagues in the class of 1988–89 always supported and encouraged me to share this idea. Special thanks to Elaine Capobianco, who assisted me in many ways. I will always be indebted to the Lucretia Crocker Academy for continuing the forum for teacher sharing.

The U.S. Department of Education awarded me the Christa McAuliffe Fellowship in 1991, which allowed me to study at the Harvard Graduate School of Education. I thank Roland Barth for inviting me to be a teaching assistant. The experience contributed to my thinking and led me to apply to the doctoral program, which led to my study of cooperating teachers as teacher educators.

I also thank Claryce Evans, my advisor in Teaching Curriculum and Learning Environments at Harvard. Her consistent support, encouragement, and good humor allowed me to maintain my vision for supporting and recognizing cooperating teachers.

A Professional Development School grant awarded through the Massachusetts Field Center for Teaching and Learning located at the University of Massachusetts–Boston allowed me to expand the concept of support for cooperating teachers. Special thanks to Karen O'Connor, Massachusetts Field Center for Teaching and Learning, University of Massachusetts–Boston and to Betty Neigum, Dickinson Public Schools, Dickinson, North Dakota, for their encouragement and for the careful editing of the first edition of this handbook.

Other educators who have contributed to this book by sharing their ideas have become good friends and professional colleagues. Thanks to Lee Teitel for his ability to keep me focused on my questions; to Gail Dion for her willingness to listen to my ideas; to Nancy Legan for her positive feedback and encouragement; and to Alice Carey for believing in my work and for the use of her Cape Cod home to write the final draft.

I am especially grateful to the teachers at the Burkland School in Middleboro, Massachusetts, who participated in all of the grants. I gratefully acknowledge Madeline Davern, who became the *Bridging the Gap* coordinator, and Amy Vena, Bridgewater State College supervisor, who worked closely with the teachers to create a team model for cooperating teachers. Thanks to all of the teachers who participated as cooperating teachers or who presented workshops for student teachers. The program would not have worked without you.

I also thank the hundreds of teachers who were willing to talk with me, answer my surveys, or give me feedback on the original handbook. These individuals include college professors, classroom teachers, student teachers, first-year teachers, and parents. All of you have contributed to this work.

My gratitude is also extended to the School of Education at Boston College, where I am currently directing the Professional Practicum Experiences program. I thank the former deans, Diana Pullin and Gerald Pine, and the current dean, Mary Brabeck, for their support and encouragement to include cooperating teachers in the teacher education programs at Boston College.

I thank Sandi Kirshner for her willingness to review the manuscript and share her ideas with Steve Dragin from Allyn and Bacon. I thank them both for their vision of the cooperating teacher as an important role in the education of future teachers.

This second edition of *A Handbook of Techniques and Strategies for Coaching Student Teachers* is a product of renewed thinking and learning that comes from active participation with student teachers, cooperating teachers, and college supervisors. Thank you to the clinical faculty at Boston College for their positive comments and suggestions that inspired activities for this new edition.

About the Author

Carol Marra Pelletier is the director of Professional Practicum Experiences at Boston College School of Education where she oversees the placement, supervision, and certification of both undergraduate and graduate students in teacher education. In more than 20 years as an elementary teacher, she received numerous awards for her work in the areas of professional development and teacher education. Her awards have included the Lucretia Crocker Fellowship sponsored by the Massachusetts Department of Education and the Christa McAuliffe Fellowship funded by the United States Department of Education. She served on the Board of Directors of the Massachusetts Teachers Association and currently serves on the Board for the Massachusetts Colleges for Teacher Education. She completed her doctoral program at the Harvard Graduate School of Education in 1996. Her dissertation, Cooperating Teachers as Teacher Educators, described four cooperating teachers' perspectives of their roles while working with student teachers. Dr. Pelletier continues to remain actively involved in collaborating with cooperating teachers, student teachers, and other field experience directors who are interested in enhancing the teacher education practicum experience.

Introduction

A Handbook of Techniques and Strategies for Coaching Student Teachers is written for any education professional who is working with beginning or preservice teachers. The first edition was the result of more than 20 years of teaching and 10 years of working with cooperating teachers and student teachers. This second edition includes specific pages for university supervisors, new forms for cooperating teachers, and a CONNECTions section that is included as part of the introduction. The completion of the second edition continues to remind us of the important role cooperating teachers, mentors, and university supervisors play as teacher educators.

The Cooperating Teacher as a Teacher Educator

Cooperating teachers are teacher educators. They have been welcoming student teachers into their classrooms for years and, in fact, provide the culminating experience for college-based teacher education programs. Cooperating teachers furnish the environment for student teachers to practice their newly acquired skills. Bridging the gap between theory and practice is complex, and yet cooperating teachers are asked to do it every time they accept a student teacher "coaching" assignment. *A Handbook of Techniques and Strategies for Coaching Student Teachers* is designed for cooperating teachers who guide and supervise student teachers.

How to Use This Handbook in Fulfilling Your Role

Working with a student teacher is one of the most important aspects of a teacher education program. Most student teachers arrive in cooperating teachers' classrooms armed with lists of activities they are supposed to complete, but few college programs give clear direction to the cooperating teacher as to how these requirements can best be met. The traditional college handbook often offers some suggestions; this handbook is designed to be used in conjunction with your student teacher's college handbook. This book offers practical strategies to enhance the experience for both the cooperating teacher and the student teacher.

As teachers, we know that every child learns differently and that there are various teaching and learning styles for all of us. This is also true for our student teachers. Many student teachers arrive with natural gifts and abilities, while others must be carefully guided to reach their full potential. This handbook serves as a guide to assist cooperating teachers in supporting both those student teachers who arrive with natural abilities for teaching and those who need more specific direction. It does not promote one right way of teaching; rather, it encourages the cooperating teacher to recognize and share diverse approaches. It is not the intent of this handbook to create clones of cooperating teachers, but to have the cooperating teachers assist the student teachers in discovering and practicing their own styles.

As a cooperating teacher, you will not be producing a finished product of a teacher; rather, you will be acting as a coach, guiding a player to discover his or her teaching style and to reach full potential. In addition to guiding the student teacher, you will find yourself reflecting on your own teaching.

This handbook may also be used by mentor teachers who are working with beginning teachers in their school districts. It can be easily adapted to the beginning teachers' situations because they were so recently student teachers. In addition, college supervisors and teacher educators at universities may find this handbook a valuable resource in preparing methods courses for student teachers. Some colleges are designing support workshops for cooperating teachers, and this could be an ideal textbook for weekly discussions about being a cooperating teacher. The book creates a common language for cooperating teachers. Although cooperating teachers most often work in isolation from other cooperating teachers, it encourages collegial conversation and sharing.

Whether one cooperating teacher uses this book with just one student teacher, or whether a group of cooperating teachers uses it together, its purpose is still to stimulate the cooperating teacher's thinking during the student teaching practicum. The handbook does not provide the "right" answer, nor is it a simple recipe for success. Using the handbook will be different every time a cooperating teacher coaches a student teacher. It is not a list of tips to be memorized that will work in all cases. It is a *process* that can be utilized each time the cooperating teacher participates in a practicum experience.

Teaching is complicated. This handbook can put some structure into your conversations with your student teacher and remind you of important topics for future discussions. In a teacher's busy life there is often not time for a discussion. The handbook provides a structure for important topics that might be missed in your daily routine. It is valuable to remind ourselves that teaching is an ongoing life experience and that we, in fact, are learning as we engage in the process of preparing a new teacher. You will have the opportunity to think about your practice as you share this book with a prospective or beginning teacher. I hope these ideas will enable you to devote more time to your conversations with your student teacher and to create some time for your own personal reflection about teaching.

A Handbook of Techniques and Strategies recognizes the importance of your role and your value as an experienced practitioner. It provides suggestions for reflection and professional growth of the cooperating teacher so that you, the classroom teacher acting in the role of cooperating teacher, can participate fully as an adult learner. Being in the role of a cooperating teacher is in itself a professional development experience; however, a more defined set of expectations for the role will enhance the experience.

You may use this book as a resource by referring to specific chapters that are of interest, or you may follow in order by chapter. The ideas and topics are not all-inclusive. The handbook is designed to stimulate further thinking that relates to your individual situation. Select the areas that will work for you and your student teacher. I suggest you share this information with the college supervisor and the student teacher, so the three of you can design an appropriate program for the practicum experience.

The ideas and suggestions in this handbook have been compiled from interviews with cooperating teachers, first-year teachers, and college faculty. I also used my own experience as a cooperating teacher to create the format for the book. The easy-to-follow structure and format should be useful and practical for cooperating teachers from pre-K–12.

Cooperating teachers, mentors, and university supervisors usually do not receive any formal training or preparation for their work with student or beginning teachers. Often, cooperating teachers come to their role with a wide variety of experiences and preparation. You may have participated in workshops or orientations to become a cooperating teacher. If you did, this handbook can be used to support those previous experiences. Whether you are a novice or an experienced cooperating teacher, this handbook will support you as you progress through the student teaching experience.

Because there is little preparation, the question often raised by cooperating teachers is: What do I do with a student teacher? This handbook serves as one way to answer that question. If there is so little preparation and often anxiety about what to do, why, then, do cooperating teachers say yes to hosting student teachers in their classrooms? There are certainly as many reasons as there are teachers. One common theme that is stated over and over is the desire to learn new things from the student teachers in order to enhance their own practice. University supervisors have also shared with me that they have learned new ideas and raised their levels of awareness as they coached their student teachers.

What is an effective cooperating teacher, mentor, or supervisor? In my experience, an important quality of an effective coach is *role understanding* of what is needed and wanted. Cooperating teachers who understand their roles, ask questions when they don't understand, and generally have a desire to be teacher educators clearly make a difference. Recognition of the role by the education community will raise the status of cooperating teachers and keep the role in the forefront of the teacher education conversation.

Another important quality of an effective cooperating teacher, mentor, or university supervisor is the human relationship required to build trust and accept the stages of a beginning teacher. A welcoming cooperating teacher who is willing to share ideas, accept new ideas, and allow a beginner to take risks creates a trusting relationship.

Finally, an effective cooperating teacher provides feedback and ongoing support throughout the practicum experience. This allows the student teacher to grow and develop while reflecting on practice. These qualities of effectiveness are highlighted in Chapter 1. What do you think makes a cooperating teacher effective?

Organization of Chapters

Each chapter begins with an overview that states the purpose of the chapter. The forms, samples, and checklists that appear throughout the chapters use the headings of **PLAN, ACT,** and **REFLECT.** The headings recognize the developmental process by which cooperating teachers coach student teachers.

This developmental process begins with **PLAN**ning, and all the forms, checklists, and samples begin with this heading. Each chapter starts with a sample lesson plan for the cooperating teacher. Other activities that involve prethinking or the design of a plan are included under this heading. Each chapter also contains a **PLAN** for university supervisors.

Cooperating teachers next have to put their **PLAN** into **ACT**ion, and **ACT** forms, checklists, and samples provide some suggestions. These action forms demonstrate the need to take one's thinking and planning further to the stage of actually doing something. These forms may include activities for the cooperating teacher, for the student teacher, or for both to do together.

After **PLAN**ning and **ACT**ion take place, most processes usually end. Many good ideas are lost simply because they have not been recorded. In this handbook, attention to **REFLECT**ion is given at the end of each chapter. **REFLECT**ion is an opportunity for both the cooperating teacher and the student teacher to review the learning process. The journal entries and the reflective questions provide a valuable opportunity for dialogue throughout the experience. Both the student teacher and the cooperating teacher may use the forms for self-assessment. Student teachers may use the journal as a documentation of the experience for a teaching portfolio; cooperating teachers may record valuable insights that might be useful in coaching future student teachers.

Chapters 1 through 16 follow the **PLAN, ACT, REFLECT** format in a developmental sequence. Each chapter closes with a Final Reminders and Helpful Hints page. Even though the handbook is designed in a sequential format from the beginning of the experience to the culmination of the practicum, each chapter can actually stand on its own. You may read the handbook in the order that suits you and your needs.

A practical note about using this handbook: You may want to three-hole punch the forms that you find you use most often and keep them in a notebook for easy reference. However, you may find yourself referring to some pages more than once; affixing self-adhesive tabs to those chapters or forms will allow you to access them quickly.

The topics selected for this book are not all-inclusive. Feel free to add your own topics and areas of interest to share with your student teacher. The handbook is not designed to maintain the status quo in education, but to have effective practice shared and innovative practice discussed. If the cooperating teacher is a fully engaged member of the student teaching practicum, you and your student teacher may even create new methods together!

I am interested in your response. Please share how you have used the handbook and/or how it has met your needs by writing to me:

Carol Pelletier
Director, Professional Practicum Experiences
Boston College
135 Campion Hall
Chestnut Hill, MA 02167
e-mail: pelletca@bc.edu

CONNECTions

One role you play—whether you are a cooperating teacher, a mentor to a beginning teacher, or a university supervisor—is to "connect" your student teacher to the resources available. As you proceed through this handbook, use this list as a guide to *making connections* that provide your beginner with information about the teaching profession. Feel free to add any of your own personal connections!

CONNECT with People: *Consider contacting any of the following people throughout the practicum to learn more about the school or to gain insight into the teaching profession.*

- Favorite teachers you or your student teacher have known (to gain advice and tips)

- Other student teachers (to create support groups of beginners)

- Educational support staff in the building (to learn other aspects of school life)

- Students in the school (to learn what students like about this school)

- Other teachers in the building (to observe and share ideas)

- Parents of students through parent organizations (to gain perspective)

- Guidance counselors, school psychologists, school nurse (to learn how school works)

- Community members, business owners, and neighbors of the school (to learn views)

- Administrators and department chairs (to learn how to be evaluated)

- The College Practicum Experiences Office or the college support services people (to assist in a variety of areas)
- Other people?

CONNECT with Professional Organizations: *To discover what they offer as services to teachers and how you would benefit by being a member, consult the following professional organizations.*

- National Education Association (NEA) or American Federation of Teachers (AFT)
- State and local teacher associations and unions
- Professional organizations in your subject area
- County associations
- Other groups for teachers?

CONNECT with Reading and Resources: *Consider the following resources to be aware, review, or use throughout the practicum or in the beginning years of teaching.*

- Professional magazines and journals in your field or at your grade level
- Authors writing about schools and instructional practice, such as:

    Danielson: *Enhancing Professional Practice*

    Roe and Ross: *Student Teaching and Field Experiences Handbook*

    Barth: *Improving Schools from Within*

    Airasian and Gullickson: *Teacher Self-Evaluation Tool Kit*

    Pitton: *Stories of Student Teaching*

    Chase and Chase: *Tips from the Trenches*

    Also consider these authors: Eleanor Duckworth, Vivian Paley, Shirley Brice Heath, Beverly Tatum, and add your own: _____

    Also consider searching for books and article on these topics: diverse learners, technology and teaching, assessment, classroom management, discipline, creating a teacher portfolio, and your own ideas: _____

CONNECT with Technology: *Discover the following technology to enhance your student teaching experience.*

- Use Amazon.com to review books and authors and to discover other resources.

- Use the computer to write your feedback for the student teacher.

- Use e-mail to communicate and maintain a dialogue with your student teacher.

- Discover websites for new ideas, lesson plans, support groups, and anything related to teaching at your grade level. Try these:

    www.edweek.org

    www.educationworld.com

    www.teachingeducation.com

    Teachnet.com

    www.eagle.ca

    www.nea.org

- Use the Internet to support the curriculum in your classroom.

- Use the Internet for a job search.

Interacting with Your Student Teacher

Each of the nine chapters in this section includes forms, checklists, and questions that help the cooperating teacher *PLAN, ACT,* and *REFLECT* on the student teaching experience. Each of these chapter ends with a page that contains Final Reminders and Helpful Hints.

Student teaching is a collaborative effort between the cooperating teacher and the student teacher. Building a relationship between you and your student teacher is an integral part of the process. A cooperating teacher can be considered a coach for a beginning teacher. A coach has valuable information to offer but also recognizes the skills of the player. A relationship built on trust and honest feedback is one that will be valued by both participants. This is easier said than done. This section offers the idea of collaborating with your student teacher as a means to a more powerful learning experience for both of you.

The chapters in this section focus on areas where a cooperating teacher would be interacting with a student teacher. Select the areas you find most useful as you begin your relationship with your student teacher.

CHAPTER 1

Preparing for Your Student Teacher

Chance favors the prepared mind.
Louis Pasteur

This chapter is designed to organize the cooperating practitioner's thoughts and materials before the student teacher arrives in the building. Careful *preplanning* will set the stage for a positive experience. It will also bring any questions you have to the forefront right away so that the college supervisor can assist you in this preparation process.

The forms, samples, and checklists in this chapter will help you prepare for this experience as you anticipate your student teacher's arrival. New beginnings are exciting.

Lesson Plan

Time: Prior to meeting the student teacher

Title: Preparing for Your Student Teacher

Purpose: To get mentally and physically organized for the student teaching experience

Objectives:
- To set goals and responsibilities
- To organize the classroom
- To prepare a "survival packet " (see ACT 1-4) for student teacher
- To meet with the college supervisor
- To review the college handbook

Needs/Materials: College handbook

Desk and chair for student teacher

Survival packet of information

Procedure:
1. Set up a place in the room for the student teacher.
2. Write specific responsibilities (see ACT 1-5).
3. Organize all pertinent information into a survival packet.
4. Call the student teacher and the supervisor to set times to meet.

**Other Thoughts/
Notes/Questions:** Talk with other cooperating teachers to gather ideas that may be useful. Keep a journal or notebook with these ideas. Ask yourself: What can I offer a student teacher? How can I be an effective coach? How can the students in my classroom gain from a student teacher? What do I want to gain from this experience?

University Supervisor Suggestions

PLAN: Organize your thoughts and materials, and prepare for your role.

Key Questions

1. Why do you want to supervise student teachers?

2. How have you prepared yourself to work with preservice teachers?

Teaching Competency Focus Areas for Chapter 1

Knowledge, Communication, Instructional Practice, Evaluation, Problem Solving, Equity, **& Professionalism**

CONNECT: Use resources to enhance your skills as a supervisor.

People. Who is supervising *you*? Check in with that person to review your role.

Books and Resources. Read current certification requirements and college handbooks.

Technology. Discover websites! Try www.edweek.org to get started.

ACT: Select the activities that will be useful to you or create your own.

ACTion #1. Review job description and responsibilities.

ACTion #2. Write goals for the semester. What do you hope to achieve?

ACTion #3. Partner with another supervisor to share ideas.

> **REFLECT:** **Think about your role as a supervisor and write a one-page reflection.**

Choose to respond to the key questions on the previous page, create a prompt of your own, or answer the following question: How are you feeling right now as you prepare to meet your student teacher?

Cooperating Teacher Profile

Give this completed form to your student teacher at your first meeting. Other information to share might include (1) your philosophy of education, (2) current professional development activities in which you are participating, (3) a description of your current curriculum, (4) your style of teaching, and (5) a description of your classroom.

Name: _____ **School:** _____

Address: _____

_____ **Phone:** _____

1. How many years have you been teaching in your present assignment?

_____

2. How many total years have you been teaching? List all grade levels and subject areas you have taught.

_____

_____

3. Have you ever been a cooperating teacher? If yes, list the number of times and dates. If no, share why not.

_____

_____

4. List your strengths and skills that will contribute to your work with a student teacher.

_____

_____

5. Share why you are looking forward to being a cooperating teacher.

_____

_____

8

Ideas for the Student Teacher Survival Packet

This packet or notebook should be prepared before the student teacher formally begins the practicum. It may be given to the student teacher at your introductory meeting. Gather the information and place it in a three-ring binder so other information can be added later. If you do not have time to organize everything, give the materials to the student teacher loose and ask him or her to review all the information and put it in a binder for the first day of school. Information for the Survival Packet could include the following:

SAMPLE SURVIVAL ITEMS

- [ ] School and student handbooks with mission statements and policies
- [ ] Curriculum guides and textbooks with teacher editions
- [ ] Daily schedules
- [ ] Class lists and seating charts for students and faculty list of teachers and other staff
- [ ] Fire drill and building-evacuation procedures
- [ ] Students with special needs or health issues (e.g., first aid and medications)
- [ ] Sample of report card and progress reports
- [ ] Map of school with room numbers for location of copy room, restrooms, faculty room, and library
- [ ] Policies for communication with parents—any special forms required
- [ ] Discipline policies for school and classroom—written and informal procedures
- [ ] Guidelines for referring students to principal—forms and expectations
- [ ] Supervisory duties during the school day (e.g., cafeteria, hall duty, study hall, etc.)
- [ ] Policies for reporting child abuse, neglect, and other legal issues—state laws
- [ ] Professional development opportunities during student teaching
- [ ] Procedures for supporting/assisting at-risk students
- [ ] Other?
- [ ] Other?

Effective Cooperating Teacher Skills:
What Should You Strive For?

Studies have shown that the cooperating teacher is the most important part of a successful student teaching experience. Being a cooperating teacher is a complex role, and if it is your first time, the task can be daunting. Use the following topics to guide you as you think about your role as a cooperating teacher. Add your own ideas!

1. Content Knowledge

GUIDELINES FOR THE EFFECTIVE COOPERATING TEACHER

1. Demonstrate love of the content area(s) and assist the student teacher in making personal connections with the students.

2. Share the curriculum materials and textbooks available for use and guide the student teacher in how to use them most effectively.

3. Refer the student teacher to resources that will enhance content and encourage him or her to use a variety of resources when teaching content.

2. Instructional Practice and Equity

GUIDELINES FOR THE EFFECTIVE COOPERATING TEACHER

1. Model, share, and demonstrate lesson plans and approaches to teaching and learning, and provide opportunities for the student teacher to try on her or his own.

2. Assist the student teacher in developing and maintaining a classroom that is well managed and organized to meet the objectives for student learning.

3. Discuss controversial issues and provide time for the student teacher to reflect on practice and the effect of a teacher's influence on students.

4. Model fair and equitable treatment of all students.

5. Stress the importance of noninstructional duties and share these duties with the student teacher.

3. Student Assessment

GUIDELINES FOR THE EFFECTIVE COOPERATING TEACHER

1. Assist the student teacher in learning about all students in the classroom.

2. Discuss and share all models of assessment for students, including special education, informal and formal teacher tests, rubrics, state tests, and how to use the results to plan and design curriculum.

3. Provide opportunities for the student teacher to create assessment tools.

4. Communication, Conferencing, and Feedback

GUIDELINES FOR THE EFFECTIVE COOPERATING TEACHER

1. Maintain a positive "mentor" approach to guiding the student teacher, demonstrating the qualities of enthusiasm, encouragement, and patience.

2. Accept the student teacher as a partner in the classroom and introduce him or her to students in the classroom as a co-teacher.

3. Develop a trusting environment open to the sharing of ideas and personal philosophies related to teaching and learning.

4. Meet with the student teacher regularly to discuss planning and other issues.

5. Provide ongoing feedback verbally and in writing to assess the student teacher's strengths and areas that need attention.

6. Encourage and participate in ongoing reflection with the student teacher.

7. Offer suggestions for areas that need assistance and set specific goals related to those areas.

5. Professionalism

GUIDELINES FOR THE EFFECTIVE COOPERATING TEACHER

1. Demonstrate a commitment to the profession and to your student teacher by behavior, personal appearance, speech, and manner.

2. Participate in professional development activities and encourage the student teacher to be a life-long learner

3. Maintain a positive relationship with colleagues, parents, and administrators, and introduce the student teacher to the whole school.

6. Other

GUIDELINES FOR THE EFFECTIVE COOPERATING TEACHER

What are other guidelines you believe an effective cooperating teacher should follow?

1. _____

_____

2. _____

_____

3. _____

_____

Expectations for the Practicum

Star those activities you feel are absolutely essential to a quality teaching experience. Check those you feel would be helpful for your student teacher. Add your own activities that pertain to your particular grade level or subject area in the space provided.

SAMPLE *PROCESS-RELATED* ACTIVITIES

_____ Visit other classrooms and special area teachers to observe teachers and teaching styles.

_____ Use duplicating equipment/computers/technology, and so on.

_____ Participate in teacher duty schedule/study halls/playground duties, and so on.

_____ Review student records for special needs.

_____ Attend parent conferences and observe the cooperating teacher.

_____ Correct and assess student work in a variety of ways.

_____ Attend faculty meetings with the cooperating teacher.

_____ Participate in professional development with the cooperating teacher.

SAMPLE *PRODUCT-RELATED* ACTIVITIES

_____ Maintain a planbook and/or lesson plans.

_____ Create a learning center/bulletin board/teacher-made game, and so on.

_____ Design a curriculum unit of study/theme unit/integrated unit, and so on.

_____ Organize a portfolio of student work samples/collection of student essays, and so on.

_____ Collect samples of assessment/teacher-made tests/portfolio assessment process, and so on.

_____ Keep a journal/reflections/diary.

_____ Create a videotape or audiotape of a lesson.

_____

_____

_____

List other expectations you have for the practicum experience.

_____ _____

_____ _____

_____ _____

_____ _____

_____ _____

_____ _____

_____ _____

Share this list with your college supervisor and cooperating teacher.

Before You Meet Your Student Teacher

Check when completed.

_____ 1. List your goals and expectations for the practicum experience (to be shared at your first meeting) (see Chapter 2).

_____

_____

_____

_____

_____

_____ 2. Organize an area in your room for your student teacher. Obtain an extra teacher's desk and start collecting books and materials for him or her to use. List the materials you need to find for your student teacher.

_____

_____

_____

_____ 3. Prepare a Student Teacher Survival Packet or notebook that contains pertinent information such as seating plans, class lists, room rules, school rules, schedules, fire drill procedures, grading policies, course curriculums or syllabi, and so on.

_____ 4. Make a copy of your responsibilities to the student teacher and share at the first meeting.

_____ 5. Think about how you will introduce the student teacher to the students. (Introductions as *teachers* or *coteachers* give student teachers more credibility.)

Sample Letter to Your Colleagues

Date: _____

Dear Colleagues,

On September 3, my student teacher, Karen Roberts, will be arriving for her 16-week practicum. I am looking forward to the experience and I have started to organize my materials to share with her. Please drop by and say hello.

I would like her to observe as many teachers in the building as possible during her first few weeks here. I believe she can gain valuable knowledge by observing many different teaching styles. Would you be willing to have her observe one of your classes? Let me know if you would be interested.

A welcome breakfast is being planned for the morning of her first day. It will be held in the teachers' lounge, and the principal has agreed to provide donuts and coffee.

I consider preparing a student teacher a "team" experience, and I welcome your ideas in assisting me to share the strengths of our school.

Please join me in welcoming Karen to our staff.

Sincerely,

Sample Letter to Parents

Date: _____

Dear Parents,

Our class is very fortunate to have Patrick Cunningham from State University join us as he begins his student teaching. The Mayflower Public Schools have always been involved in the preparation of teachers, and this is another opportunity for our school and classroom to experience the enthusiasm of a beginning professional teacher.

Having a student teacher participate in our classroom allows the students to experience a variety of teaching methods. It also provides our classroom with two teachers, so more individual attention may be given to the students. Many of the lessons will be cotaught with me. Please be assured that I will be working cooperatively with Mr. Cunningham and all activities and lessons will be supervised by me. If you have any questions, do not hesitate to call me.

Mr. Cunningham will be attending at our school Open House next week. Please join me in welcoming him to our staff for the fall term.

Sincerely,

Questions? Questions? Questions?

List any questions you have and refer them to the appropriate person.

QUESTIONS FOR THE COLLEGE SUPERVISOR

Examples: What is the length of the practicum? Will my student teacher be released for any special meetings? How can I communicate with you? Are there any special requirements? Did you ever have this student teacher in an academic class? What is your experience as a supervisor? How can we work together as a team to assist this student teacher?

1. _____

2. _____

3. _____

4. _____

5. _____

QUESTIONS FOR THE STUDENT TEACHER

Examples: What are you most excited about? What are your biggest fears? How can I be most helpful to you during the practicum? Have you had any previous teaching experience? What is the best way to communicate with you after school hours? (These questions may be asked at the first meeting. Other questions can be added to the Student Teacher's Profile (ACT 2-7).)

1. _____

2. _____

3. _____

4. _____

5. _____

Cooperating Teacher's Reflection

It is important to assess the student teaching experience as you go along. If you wait until the end of the practicum, you may forget valuable information that will be useful the next time you coach a student teacher.

JOURNAL ENTRY

What has stood out for you as you prepared for the arrival of your student teacher?

Date: _____

_____

_____

_____

_____

_____

REFLECTIVE QUESTIONS

1. What did you find difficult or easy as you prepared for your student teacher?

_____

_____

2. What will you do differently next time you prepare for a student teacher?

_____

_____

3. What kinds of support did you find most helpful as you prepared for your student teacher? What kind of support did you need as you prepared?

_____

_____

Final Reminders and Helpful Hints

Careful planning will set the stage for a positive experience. Planning makes a difference!

_____ Have your students write letters to the student teacher to introduce themselves. This learning experience for the class provides valuable firsthand information about each student. A videotape, audiotape, or class photographs can also serve as an introduction.

_____ Meet or talk with the college supervisor before the student teacher arrives. Be sure to share your goals and expectations with the college supervisor.

_____ Inform your colleagues that a student teacher is arriving and ask if they would be available to be observed or interviewed.

_____ Let the office secretary and custodian know you will have a student teacher. They can help provide the resources (e.g., desk, planbook, grade book, etc.) you will need.

_____ Plan a welcome breakfast to introduce the student teacher to the entire staff.

_____ Invite the principal to meet with the student teacher.

_____ Call the college to get a handbook if you do not have one and ask for the supervisor's name and phone number.

_____ Call and make an appointment to have your first meeting with your student teacher.

_____ List your own helpful hints:

_____

_____

_____

CHAPTER 2

First Meeting with Your Student Teacher

When schemes are laid in advance, it is surprising how often the circumstances fit in with them.

William Osler

This chapter is designed to prepare you for a successful and informative first meeting with your student teacher. First meetings and first impressions are always important, so make sure you are not rushed. Set the tone for a pleasant professional conversation. At *least* an hour should be set aside for this meeting in a location free of interruptions. Allowing the student teacher to contribute to the conversation and to share his or her ideas and goals for the experiences should be a goal of the meeting.

This is your opportunity to share the survival packet you have prepared, the goals you have listed, and your list of responsibilities as you see them. Any textbooks, curriculum guides, or school-related information should be given to the student teacher at this time. It is also an opportunity to discuss his or her goals and to compare them with yours. The Student Teacher Profile can be given to the student teacher to be returned later, or it can be a guide for discussion.

Create a partnership with the student teacher at this first meeting. Be "up front" and honest about responsibilities and the quality of work you will expect. Let the student teacher share his or her thoughts and concerns about the upcoming experience and work out any problems or concerns that may be on the student teacher's mind. Ask the relevant questions that you prepared in Chapter 1.

Remind the student teacher that you see yourself as a coach and that you are available for support and encouragement throughout the experience.

The forms, samples, and checklists in this chapter will help you prepare for a successful first meeting and will assist you in creating clarification of expectations, which will prevent confusion.

Lesson Plan

Time: Before the practicum begins

Title: First Meeting with the Student Teacher

Purpose: To create a partnership with the student teacher and share expectations, information, and resources

Objectives:
- To personally get acquainted
- To discuss responsibilities
- To do goal-setting process
- To orient the student teacher to the classroom/school
- To review the college handbook (i.e., requirements)
- To share the packet you prepared

Materials: College handbook

Packet you prepared

Letters from students in your class to the student teacher

Textbooks, plan book, curriculum guides

Refreshments, tea/coffee (optional)

Procedure:
1. Have an informal conversation and share profiles.
2. Set goals (ask the student teacher to do this at home).
3. Review college requirements.

4. Share your expectations and goals.

5. Handle problems, concerns, and questions.

6. Orient the student teacher to the room and school.

**Other Thoughts/
Notes:** Ask the student teacher to take the packet home and read through

it.

University Supervisor Suggestions

PLAN: Organize your thoughts and materials, and prepare for your role.

Key Questions

1. How will your organize your first meeting?

2. What do you need to know and be able to do to assist the student teacher?

Teaching Competency Focus Areas for Chapter 2

Knowledge, **Communication**, Instructional Practice, Evaluation, Problem Solving, Equity, & **Professionalism**

CONNECT: Use resources to enhance your skills as a supervisor.

People.   Who are key people at the school site? Meet them all!

Books and Resources.   Review any current student teaching handbooks and texts.

Technology.   Use the Internet to discover the latest books in the field. Try amazon.com

ACT: Select the activities that will be useful to you or create your own.

ACTion #1.   Review school, cooperating teacher, and community profiles.

ACTion #2.   Discuss all requirements at a three-way meeting (you, the student teacher, and the cooperating teacher).

ACTion #3.   Decide who will mediate if any issues arise during the practicum.

REFLECT: Think about your role as a supervisor and write a one-page reflection.

Choose to respond to the key questions on the previous page, create a prompt of your own, or answer the following question: What are your first impressions of the student teacher, the cooperating teacher, and the school?

Checklist: Discussion Ideas for the First Meeting

Check the topics you feel are most important to discuss at the first meeting. Use this as a guide to share other items later.

_____ Discuss the basic responsibilities of the student teacher.

_____ Share your responsibilities to the student teacher.

_____ Orient the student teacher to the classroom.

_____ Give the student teacher a tour of the school.

_____ Review college requirements and the college handbook.

_____ Briefly review any relevant special calendar dates.

_____ Discuss daily routine, schedules, duties, and so on.

_____ Review lesson plan formats; select one later.

_____ Discuss possible feedback strategies.

_____ Review self-evaluation/reflection options.

_____ Discuss the appropriate dress code for the student teacher.

_____ Share the discipline code for the classroom and the school.

_____ Discuss the substitute policy for the student teacher.

_____ Discuss dates of the practicum and the attendance policy.

_____

_____

_____

_____

_____

Building a Relationship:
The Supervisor and the Cooperating Teacher as a Team

There are many details involved in supervising a student teacher. Whether you are an experienced cooperating teacher or a supervisor, you still need to review and update current requirements together to ensure consistency. Working as a team is essential to building a strong working relationship. Use the following ideas to guide your work together:

- List your expectations for the practicum.

- What questions do you have as you begin this experience?

- Have a one-on-one meeting with the student teacher. Use this time to communicate your expectations, ask and answer questions, and clarify all procedures. Exchange home phone numbers. Discuss the grading policies and the requirement expectations from the college.

- Schedule all three-way meetings for the semester and discuss the purpose of each meeting. The supervisor should explain what will be expected at each meeting and how the cooperating teacher will participate. Forms, paperwork, and more forms are typically required. Show and discuss each form and how it will be used to document growth.

- Discuss the role of the cooperating teacher during scheduled observations. Should the teacher stay in the room? Leave the room? Stay for part of the lesson? Should it vary?

Sample Agenda for the First Meeting

Date: _____ Time: _____ Location: _____

1. Introductions/Light Refreshments/Coffee/Juice

    A. Sharing general information

    B. Questions

2. Sharing Information/Ideas

    A. College requirements

    B. School packet/notebook prepared earlier

    C. Letters from classroom students

3. Goals and Expectations

    A. Cooperating teacher shares goals/responsibilities

    B. Discuss goals—write them for future reference

    C. Other discussion related to practicum expectations

        1. Dress code/attendance

        2. Duties

        3. Lesson plans

    D. Student teacher completes profile at home and shares later

4. Brief Orientation to Classroom

    A. Student teacher's desk

    B. Materials/space/other information

5. Communication

    A. Set time for next meeting

    B. Exchange phone numbers (home and school)

6. Final Questions

7. School Tour

Collaborative Goal Setting

Take this meeting as an opportunity to discuss goals you have thought about as part of your preparation process. In addition, ask the student teacher to share his or her goals. It is critical to communicate your goals and to know what the student teacher has in mind. List your goals on this form and make a copy for the student teacher.

Create time during the practicum for both of you to add to/delete/and revise your goals. During the last week of the practicum, review goals on this form to see if they have been met.

EXAMPLES OF COOPERATING TEACHER GOALS

- To meet regularly with the student teacher to answer questions

- To observe the student teacher regularly

- To team teach a lesson with the student teacher

- To observe a colleague's class while the student teacher is teaching

- To try teaching some of the student teacher's lessons

- To organize curriculum materials to share with the student teacher

EXAMPLES OF STUDENT TEACHER GOALS

- To learn how to implement cooperative learning strategies effectively

- To design successful lesson plans

- To practice a variety of classroom management/discipline techniques

- To take risks in teaching new lessons

- To observe other teachers in the building

- To create an interactive learning center with manipulatives

- To incorporate lessons learned in college classes

Student Teacher Profile

Complete this profile and share it with the university supervisor and the cooperating teacher.

Name: _____ **College/University:** _____

Address: _____ **Phone:** _____

E-Mail: _____ **Major:** _____

Field of Certification: _____ **Grade Level:** _____

1. Attach your college transcript or a list of courses completed prior to student teaching to document your knowledge base in the subject(s) you will be teaching.

2. List any courses you have taken that relate to child development, adolescent psychology, and so on.

   _____

3. List your previous prepracticum experiences or other teaching experiences.

   Date of Prepracticum   School   Grade Level

   _____

   _____

   _____

4. List your skills, hobbies, and areas of expertise or interest (e.g., foreign language or travel, musical ability, drama, dance, sports, coaching, etc.).

   _____

   _____

5. Highlight all the teaching methods courses on your transcript.

6. Are you feeling emotionally ready and confident to teach this semester? _____

7. What is your commitment to the teaching profession?

Sample Letter of Introduction to Students

The style of this letter will vary, depending on the age level of the students. Primary students could receive a large "big book"–style letter; older students could have a more formal, traditional letter form. The cooperating teacher should share the letter with the students before the student teacher arrives.

Date: _____

Dear Students in Room 2,

My name is Maria Sanchez and I will be student teaching with Mrs. Jones for the next 16 weeks. I am completing my senior year at State University with a double major of history and education. I have taken several exciting courses in archeology and I thought it would be interesting to share this information with you.

I have traveled to several different parts of the United States, and I collect artifacts of Native Americans, particularly Southwestern Native Americans. I hope to design several history lessons that relate to this topic.

I decided to become a teacher because I like my subject area and sharing it with others. I've taught museum programs for students and summer YMCA extension courses already.

Mrs. Jones and I will be working together to make this a positive learning experience for all of you. I look forward to meeting you next Monday.

Sincerely,

Cooperating Teacher's Reflection

After you meet with your student teacher, write your first impressions. Save this journal to see if your impressions are the same at the end of the experience.

JOURNAL ENTRY

What was your overall impression of the first meeting?

Date: _____

_____

_____

_____

_____

REFLECTIVE QUESTIONS

Thinking about Your First Meeting. Take a moment to record your thoughts by answering these questions. Your answers may help other cooperating teachers or be useful reminders to your future work with student teachers.

1. What would you do differently next time?

_____

_____

2. What would you be sure to do the same?

_____

_____

3. What needs to be done at a future meeting?

_____

_____

Final Reminders and Helpful Hints

_____ Select a limited number of items to discuss at the first meeting. You cannot cover everything in one meeting, so select your priority items.

_____ Set a time limit for the meeting. One hour is the minimum—two hours would be more realistic. Beforehand, tell the student teacher how long the meeting will be.

_____ The information you share will seem overwhelming to the student teacher. Try to select the most appropriate information for the beginning of the experience, and add other information later.

_____ Remember—the more you say about your expectations and goals, the fewer problems and misunderstandings you will have later.

_____ Do not forget to exchange phone numbers.

_____ At your first meeting, set up a time to meet again and answer any questions the student teacher may have.

_____ Keep the college supervisor informed.

_____ List your own reminders and hints:

_____

_____

_____

_____

_____

_____

CHAPTER 3

Designing a Plan for the Practicum

We will either find a way or make one.
Hannibal

The purpose of this chapter is to provide a means for you and your student teacher to plan the practicum experience together. It is important for the student teacher to be able to see the *end* of the experience from the beginning. The length of student teaching experiences varies. This planning skill is a necessary one for student teachers as they learn to judge the time it takes to start and complete individual lessons and units of study.

The planning process may have to be done several times during the experience, because plans and intentions may change. Use pencil so that the form can be easily erased. Allow the student teacher to update, revise, or delete as the term moves along. The plan should be done in partnership so as not to interfere with the curriculum that needs to be accomplished. The forms, checklists, and samples in this chapter will assist you in designing an effective plan that allows your student teacher time to observe you "on stage" and gives you opportunities to coach from "back stage."

Lesson Plan

Time: Anytime during the first week

Title: Designing a Plan for the Practicum

Purpose: To create an outline for the student teaching experience, including requirements of both college and cooperating teachers

Objectives:
- To list college requirements and classroom responsibilities
- To give suggestions for long-range planning
- To provide time-management tips
- To provide ways to document work for the future

Materials: Blank forms

Student teacher–completed goal sheet

Lists of requirements

Procedure:
1. After discussing all goals and responsibilities, set up a sequence and tentatively schedule activities.
2. Discuss time-management tips.
3. Discuss potential ways to document work.

Other Thoughts/Notes: Be flexible. Perhaps only half of the plan can be done at this meeting. If so, set up another time to complete the other half.

University Supervisor Suggestions

PLAN: Organize your thoughts and materials, and prepare for your role.

Key Questions

1. What materials, syllabi, and schedules do you need in order to design the plan?

2. What practical guidance and tips can you offer the student teacher?

Teaching Competency Focus Areas for Chapter 3

Knowledge, **Communication**, Instructional Practice, Evaluation, Problem Solving, Equity, **& Professionalism**

CONNECT: Use resources to enhance your skills as a supervisor.

People. If there is more than one cooperating teacher, share requirements with all.

Books and Resources. Read *Teacher's Survival Guide* by Warner and Bryan (Park Avenue).

Technology. Try www.eagle.ca/~matink/ for the Educator's Toolkit.

ACT: Select the activities that will be useful to you or create your own.

ACTion #1. Create a calendar that shows when all field requirements are due.

ACTion #2. Decide on observation dates, add them to your calendar, and share this information with the student teacher.

ACTion #3. Compare requirements with any other courses being taken to avoid conflicts.

REFLECT: **Think about your role as a supervisor and write a one-page reflection.**

Choose to respond to the key questions on the previous page, create a prompt of your own, or answer the following question: How do your expectations, as well as those of the student teacher and the cooperating teacher, influence the design of the practicum plan?

Sample Student Teacher Experience Checklist

Check those activities expected to be completed at the end of student teaching. List the week the activity is planned to be complete next to the checkmark. Expectations will vary by grade level.

COLLEGE REQUIREMENTS

_____ _____ Observing one student

_____ _____ Making a teacher-made test

_____ _____ Reading a story to the class/Leading a discussion group

_____ _____ Designing a unit

_____ _____ Conferencing with a student

_____ _____ Observing the cooperating teacher

_____ _____ Documenting parent communication

_____ _____ _____

_____ _____ _____

ADDITIONAL EXPECTATIONS FROM COOPERATING TEACHER

_____ _____ Maintaining an organized plan book

_____ _____ Reading books to prepare for a lesson

_____ _____ Preparing five lessons in case of absence

_____ _____ Attending parent conferences

_____ _____ Maintaining accurate assessment of student progress

_____ _____ Organizing multimedia/technology for a lesson

_____ _____ _____

_____ _____ _____

Time-Management Tips

Check the strategies you want to suggest. Add ideas from your own experience.

_____ Keep a teacher's mailbox on your desk as well as on the student teacher's desk. All assignments and notes must be put in those mailboxes.

_____ Use colors to code groups or group projects.

_____ Use precut letters for bulletin boards to save time.

_____ Have students make bulletin boards.

_____ Organize a filing system to separate papers from different classes.

_____ Assign partners to each student in the class to correct daily practice papers and to collect any missing work due to absence.

_____ List your own ideas:

_____

_____

_____

_____

_____

_____

_____

_____

_____

_____

Documenting the Student Teaching Experience

- Audiotape selected lessons.

- Collect samples of student work.

- Keep a personal daily journal.

- Videotape selected lessons.

- Write a dialogue journal with your student teacher or the supervisor. (See Reflect 3-12 for explanation of *dialogue journal*.)

- Keep a student teacher portfolio.

- List your own ideas for documentation.

_____

_____

_____

Decide together how information should be saved in an organized way throughout the practicum. Decide together what criteria should be used for selection of lessons or student samples.

DOCUMENTING OBSERVATIONS OF COOPERATING TEACHER LESSONS

Date _____   Observed lesson on _____

Comment: _____

_____

Date _____   Observed lesson on _____

Comment: _____

_____

Date _____   Observed lesson on _____

Comment: _____

_____

Looking toward Completion

List some questions to think about as the student teaching experience draws to completion.

- When will the student teacher teach full time and for how many weeks?
- Should you increase your classroom teaching the last week to ease back in while the student teacher is still there?*
- When will all assignments be due?
- When will final official paperwork for the college need to be done?

_____

_____

_____

_____

_____

_____

_____

_____

_____

_____

_____

_____

_____

Some student teachers and cooperating teachers prefer to select full weeks of teaching prior to the last week of the practicum, and during the last week they split the teaching load. This allows the student teacher some time to tie up loose ends and allows the cooperating teacher to ease back into the classroom.

Planning Calendar

	Teaching Activities	Related Activities	Requirements
Week Date			
Week Date			
Week Date			
Week Date			
Week Date			

Monthly Calendar

List significant events related to the practicum for each month the student teacher will be in your classroom. Copy the calendar page as needed, filling in the dates for the school days.

Month: _____						
Mon.	*Tues.*	*Wed.*	*Thur.*	*Fri.*	*Sat.*	*Sun.*

Weekly Planning Form

Monday
  Lesson topic:

  Skill:

Tuesday
  Lesson topic:

  Skill:

Wednesday
  Lesson topic:

  Skill:

Thursday
  Lesson topic:

  Skill:

Friday
  Lesson topic:

  Skill:

Things to Do: Daily Reminders

Date: _____ Check When Completed: _____

_____ 1. _____

_____ 2. _____

_____ 3. _____

_____ 4. _____

_____ 5. _____

_____ 6. _____

_____ 7. _____

_____ 8. _____

_____ 9. _____

_____ 10. _____

_____ 11. _____

_____ 12. _____

_____

_____

_____

_____

_____

_____

_____

Student Teacher Portfolio Checklist

Documentation activities could be combined to create a portfolio the student teacher can use later for job interviews. This is just a sample of the practicum! These items could be placed in a three-ring binder or an artist's portfolio for easy sharing.

ITEMS A PORTFOLIO MIGHT CONTAIN

- Student Teacher's Profile
- Goals for teaching
- An overview of everything in the portfolio and why it was selected
- A philosophy or personal statement
- An audio or video of one lesson
- Samples of student work demonstrating a lesson taught during the semester
- Lesson plans or units designed in methods courses or during the practicum
- Letters of recommendation from you and the college supervisor

_____

_____

_____

_____

_____

_____

_____

_____

_____

Cooperating Teacher's Reflection

After the planning session with your student teacher, jot down any thoughts you have about the experience of planning together.

JOURNAL ENTRY

Date: _____

_____

_____

_____

_____

_____

_____

The following questions can be used to start a dialogue journal with the student teacher or just for private pondering. A dialogue journal is a "conversation on paper" in which the student teacher and the cooperating teacher write back and forth in one journal. The dialogue journal is successful with secondary teachers who do not have a lot of time for daily conversations with the student teacher but want to give ongoing feedback. Select one question or topic to write about or discuss.

REFLECTIVE QUESTIONS

1. What made me feel good about this planning process?

2. What has made an impression on me so far?

3. Two positive things that have happened with the student teacher.

4. How can I improve my communication with the student teacher?

5. What am I concerned about?

6. What do I have to look forward to?

7. One aspect of the planning that went very well.

Final Reminders and Helpful Hints

_____ Be flexible—allow the plan to grow and change.

_____ Use pencil to make changes more easily.

_____ Discuss the long-range plan at weekly meetings and modify and revise when necessary.

_____ Remember to add room routines to the planning calendar (e.g., collecting money, lunch count, distributing notices, and any other nonteaching assignments).

_____ Make sure all college requirements and activities you suggest are planned throughout the practicum, so they are not all being done the last week!

_____ Set aside time on a regular basis to assist the student teacher with time-management skills.

_____ Encourage the student teacher to be organized so that his or her work does not become overwhelming.

_____ List your ideas here for future reference:

_____

_____

_____

_____

_____

_____

_____

_____

_____

CHAPTER 4

Guided Observation

As I grow older, I pay less attention to what men say. I just watch what they do.

Andrew Carnegie

The purpose of this chapter is to establish the student teacher in the classroom learning environment. Observation by the student teacher is key in doing this. Rather than just looking around the room for interesting things to observe or watching every move the teacher makes, the student teacher should engage in a more planned view of the classroom. Guided observation allows the student teacher to observe what is going on in a classroom in an organized way. By setting a focus, you guide the student teacher to observe areas he or she may not ordinarily attend to in your classroom. You also create topics for discussion.

Observation is a skill that can be part of the entire practicum. After all, as an experienced teacher, you observe your students as you teach and make necessary changes as you go. Observing is a skill that is taken for granted. You might assume that the student teacher will see the interactions and the specific techniques you are modeling. Very often, this is not the case, and the only thing the student teacher gets from observing is *bored*. Observation does not have to be a boring activity that student teachers do before they are allowed to teach. It should be a carefully designed series of lessons throughout the semester that allows the student teacher to learn by seeing and recording information. It can also be a beginning step for designing teacher research in the classroom.

A student teacher not only needs to know what to look for but he or she also needs to know *how* to observe. Observing effectively takes practice on the part of the student teacher. If you feel your student teacher has not had sufficient practice during the pre-practicum, you will find the forms in this chapter helpful.

You may also want to demonstrate how observation can be done by going to a classroom with your student teacher and observing another teacher. By comparing notes, your student teacher will see how other people observe.

There are many things to focus on in an active learning environment such as the classroom. The forms in this chapter provide samples of the types of things you might want your student teacher to observe. Be clear about what you want observed and then allow him or her to observe other things, as well.

The forms, checklists, and samples will assist you as you guide your student teacher to successful observation experiences. Remember, the student teacher is observing you most of the day and this can feel stressful—like being "on stage."

Lesson Plan

Time: Beginning of the practicum

Title: Guided Observation for Your Student Teacher

Purpose: To give the student teacher the opportunity to observe other teachers and to approach observation systematically

Objectives:
- To ease the student into the classroom
- To encourage the observation of several teachers
- To build on prepracticum observation skills and refine observation techniques

Materials: Forms in this chapter

Procedure:
1. Discuss options for observing other teachers.
2. Write a letter to colleagues.
3. Assist in setting up observations.
4. Select some forms to use in observing.
5. Reflect and share observations.

Other Thoughts/ Notes: Find out how skilled the student teacher is in observing a learning environment. Suggest that the student teacher follow one student from the large classroom situation to a smaller group to see the different ways a student will interact.

University Supervisor Suggestions

PLAN: Organize your thoughts and materials, and prepare for your role.

Key Questions

1. How can you support the student teacher in using guided observation to enhance his or her learning experiences in the classroom?

2. How will the student teacher share these observation forms with you?

Teaching Competency Focus Areas for Chapter 4

Knowledge, Communication, **Instructional Practice**, Evaluation, Problem Solving, Equity, & Professionalism

CONNECT: Use resources to enhance your skills as a supervisor.

People. Who would your student teacher like to observe?

Books and Resources. Use current supervision research and techniques to guide you.

Technology. Try the websites titled *Teacher Talk* and *Education World*.

ACT: Select the activities that will be useful to you or create your own.

ACTion #1. Review pages in this text and discuss observation forms with the student teacher.

ACTion #2. Share the benefits of guided observation with the student teacher.

ACTion #3. Create a new type of guided observation activity for your student teacher.

REFLECT: Think about your role as a supervisor and write a one-page reflection.

> Choose to respond to the key questions on the previous page, create a prompt of your own, or answer the following question: What are your first impressions of the student teacher, cooperating teacher, and the schools?

Sample Letter to Colleagues

Date: _____

Dear Colleagues,

I believe a basic part of a positive learning experience for a student teacher involves observing other teachers and teaching styles. Student teachers can gain valuable insights and observe that many types of teachers make up a school. As this student teacher begins to discover his style and philosophy, I believe it is important to have him observe as many teachers as possible. Would you be willing to invite Brian Baker into your classroom for a period so he may benefit from viewing another teacher in action?

Brian will be using forms from the second edition of *A Handbook of Techniques and Strategies for Coaching Student Teachers* to collect data and answer questions to help him focus his observation. If you would like to see the forms, please see me and I would be happy to share them prior to the observation.

Let me know if you are willing and the dates and times an observation would be welcome. Thank you!

Sincerely,

What Should the Student Teacher Be Looking For?

There are a multitude of things to look for in a classroom. As in looking under a microscope, things do not become clear until you focus. Check the items you feel your student teacher should examine at one time or another during the practicum. He or she can look at these specific aspects in addition to the focus on the teacher, individual child, or whole class.

1. Classroom Management

_____ A. Physical organization of classroom

_____ B. Pacing of lesson

_____ C. Beginning and ending of lesson

_____ D. Monitoring of students

_____ E. Traffic flow of classroom

_____ F. Routines and procedures used

_____ G. Structure of lesson

2. Instructional Strategies

_____ A. Instructional practices used (lecture? cooperative? combination?)

_____ B. Teaching materials and audiovisuals

_____ C. Technology use incorporated into lesson

3. Classroom Environment

_____ A. Teacher's "style" (description?)

_____ B. Interactions with students

_____ C. Engagement of students with diverse needs

_____ D. Positive reinforcement

_____ E. Handling of disruptions

4. Lesson Plan

_____ A. Presence of lesson plan

_____ B. Fit of the plan as part of a unit into the bigger picture

_____ C. Clarity of curriculum objectives for learning

5. Assessment of Lesson

_____ A. Formal assessment

_____ B. Informal assessment

6. Other

_____ _____

_____ _____

_____ _____

_____ _____

Strategies for Observation

Collecting data in the classroom is one way to observe what is happening. After data collection, the student teacher should meet with the cooperating teacher to interpret what was seen.

STRATEGY 1: NOTE TAKING

While observing, the student teacher should write down what is happening. This can also include what the student teacher hears. For example, he or she may write all the questions you asked during a given period or write how one student responded during the entire lesson. This is often called *scripting a lesson*. (If more than one student teacher is in your building, they could observe in pairs or small groups and discuss information observed after observation.)

STRATEGY 2: STUDENT/TEACHER INTERACTION

During the observation, the student teacher, using a seating chart, draws lines showing who in the classroom was called on and how many times different students spoke. This will also show how much the teacher is talking and if there is any tendency toward gender bias. Cooperating teachers often use student teachers to assist them in discovering details of their teaching styles.

STRATEGY 3

List one of your strategies here:

_____

_____

_____

_____

_____

_____

_____

Being Observed by Your Student Teacher

The practicum experience is designed to provide opportunities for student teachers to practice their methods and to reflect on their roles as teachers. A major part of the experience relates to observation of students, the school culture, and you, the cooperating teacher. Being observed on a daily basis, even at an informal level by a beginner, can be uncomfortable. In fact, many cooperating teachers have shared that they have initially refused to having a student teacher in the room because they would feel nervous having someone watching them teach all day long. How can you use this observation time as a learning experience for your student teacher?

THINGS TO THINK ABOUT

1. How do you respond to being observed? Formally? Informally?

_____

_____

2. Do you like to have other adults in the classroom? Why or why not?

_____

_____

3. When was the last time an adult was in your classroom?

_____

_____

Preparing to Be Observed: Creating a Learning Experience

Before the Observation	Share the lesson objective with the student teacher.	Ask the student teacher to watch for certain things.
During the Observation	Highlight aspects of your teaching as you go along.	Ask the student teacher to write questions to ask after the observation.
After the Observation	Meet to discuss the lesson.	Ask the student teacher what he or she observed.

Observing a Teacher

Name of Teacher: _____ **Date:** _____

Subject Area/Grade: _____

Specific Observation for: _____

If this is not your room, sketch the set-up of the classroom and save for future reference.

1. How would you describe the teacher's style of presenting a lesson?

   _____

   _____

2. What materials or resources were used in the lesson? Technology? Media?

   _____

   _____

3. How did the teacher maintain interest throughout the lesson?

   _____

   _____

4. How was the lesson culminated?

   _____

   _____

5. How do you know the students learned anything?

   _____

   _____

6. Write your own questions and answers on an additional sheet.

Observing a Student

Date: _____ First Name of Student: _____

Grade/Subject: _____

1. What do you notice about this student (physical appearance, cultural background, language, social interaction, skills and abilities, motivation, attitude, self-concept, etc.)?

   _____

   _____

2. How is the student responding to the teacher's lesson?

   _____

   _____

3. Is the student interacting with any other students? Describe.

   _____

   _____

4. What is the quality of the student's work?

   _____

   _____

5. Name something positive the student did during the lesson.

   _____

   _____

6. What other things did you observe?

   _____

   _____

Observing a Small Group

Date: _____ **Number in Group:** _____

Subject/ Grade Level: _____ **Teacher:** _____

1. Why is this small group working together?

   _____

2. Who is the leader of the group? Is the leader self-appointed or teacher-appointed?

   _____

3. How effective is the leader?

   _____

4. Is the group completing the assigned task? How do you know?

   _____

5. Are all members of the group participating? What are the differences in the individual members' contributions to the group? Give an example.

   _____

6. What is your overall impression of this group activity?

   _____

7. Write any questions you have.

   _____

Observing a Whole Classroom

Date: _____ Teacher: _____

Grade Level/Subject: _____

Sketch the classroom and how students are seated and attach to this form.

1. How would you describe the students in this classroom?

_____

_____

2. Note the number of students responding to the teacher and the number who are not. Why do you think this is happening?

_____

_____

3. Do you notice any individual differences among the students? How do you know? Why do you think that?

_____

_____

4. Describe an effective teaching strategy the teacher used.

_____

_____

5. How would you describe the classroom environment? Does it facilitate learning? How do you know?

_____

_____

Cooperating Teacher's Reflection

JOURNAL ENTRY

How did the observation process work?

Date: _____

_____

_____

_____

_____

_____

_____

REFLECTIVE QUESTIONS

1. In designing the observation lessons for my student teacher, what have I learned?

_____

_____

2. What worked really well?

_____

_____

3. How do I observe my own classroom while I am teaching?

_____

_____

Final Reminders and Helpful Hints

_____ Observe the student teacher before assigning all these observation forms. Adjust your expectations to the student teacher's needs. All forms do not have to be done at once; they can be spread out through the semester.

_____ Talk with the supervisor about how much prepracticum experience the student teacher already has had in observation. Adapt your plan as needed.

_____ Remember to include special-area teachers (e.g., art, music, special needs, guidance, etc.) as practitioners the student can observe.

_____ Crossing grade-level and subject-area boundaries for observations is beneficial. The student teacher can still pick up teaching strategies, management techniques, and so on.

_____ Encourage the student teacher to collect in a file box or loose-leaf notebook all the good ideas he or she observed for future teaching lessons.

_____ Assist the student teacher in utilizing the data collected to design effective teaching lessons in the future.

_____ Plan time to talk about all the information gathered.

_____ If there are two student teachers in the building, encourage them to observe together and share their learning.

_____ List your own hints for future reference:

_____

_____

_____

CHAPTER 5

Designing Lesson Plans for Effective Teaching

You can't think and hit at the same time.
Yogi Berra

Everyone involved in teacher preparation agrees that some sort of planning is essential for successful teaching at any level. A well-organized plan will assist in producing a more confident student teacher and increase the chances of a successful learning experience for the classroom students. Lesson plans are *guides* for action. A plan should not be an exhaustive process that takes away from the teaching of the lesson. Plans for student teachers should be agreed-upon steps to follow that will enhance the teaching of a lesson. Discuss the planning process with the college supervisor.

The two types of plans in this chapter include (1) long plans, or full-page descriptions of a lesson; and (2) shorter planbook-style plans, or block plans. Discuss with the supervisor how much time your student teacher should spend on completing the full-page plans before doing a shorter plan.

The emphasis should be on how well the student teacher can document the ideas in sequential order for the effective teaching of a lesson, not how well the student teacher can write a plan. *The plan is a vehicle, not the end result.* The documentation of a well–thought-out lesson plan that has been taught effectively is an excellent resource worth saving in the student teacher's portfolio.

Lesson plans are often parts of units of study or theme units. Student teachers may be required to create a series of lessons that relate and build on one another. Being able to create a thoughtful unit plan is a skill that is part of good teaching. The length of a unit may vary. However, knowing how to begin a unit, follow a sequence of lessons, and culminate the unit are all important aspects of good lesson planning.

Another part of planning is coplanning a lesson with the student teacher. It is appropriate and acceptable to assist the student teacher in the design of an effective plan. You may want to coteach several lessons you have planned together. Keep track of the lessons your student teacher has observed, assisted you with, or taught alone. This checklist will allow both of you to see at a glance where and how the student teacher is experiencing planning skills.

Set a mutually agreeable time to review the student teacher's lesson plans *before* he or she teaches. The written plan alone is not the only indicator of a successful lesson. The successful delivery of a plan is essential, also. Delivery is discussed in the next chapter.

Finally, decide how you want to handle self-evaluation. Do you want to include it as part of each lesson plan, or have it be a weekly process that includes all lessons? Some forms include self-evaluation because the student teacher wants to be able to compare his or her thoughts with any feedback from the cooperating teacher. The self-evaluation comments can be useful for future planning and making any adjustments when the lesson is taught again.

The forms, checklists, and samples in this chapter will help you and your student teacher select an appropriate format to follow when planning lessons. Letting go of your classes and students can often be an issue for cooperating teachers. Use this chapter to guide your planning and note when the student teacher will teach.

Lesson Plan

Time: Beginning of the practicum

Title: Lesson Plans and Units

Purpose: To demonstrate that good planning is a guide for effective teaching

Objectives:
- To decide what the important parts of a plan are and to share your plan book
- To distinguish between long and short plans
- To set a time for checking the student teacher's plans
- To select or design a plan together
- To share a unit or theme plan process

Procedure:
1. Discuss the philosophy of good planning.
2. Talk with the supervisor about expectations.
3. Create a form or select one from the samples.
4. Set a time to check plans daily/weekly.
5. Establish a time line for long plan forms.

Other Thoughts/ Notes: Write a long plan for a lesson you are teaching and show it to the student teacher before the lesson. Let the student teacher follow you through the plan as you teach. Talk about the lesson after you teach it. Compare the plan to what you actually did. Were there any differences? Explain to the student teacher why this might happen.

University Supervisor Suggestions

> **PLAN:** Organize your thoughts and materials, and prepare for your role.

Key Questions

1. How does good planning affect teaching and learning?

2. How will you share planning options with your student teacher?

Teaching Competency Focus Areas for Chapter 5

Knowledge, Communication, **Instructional Practice**, Evaluation, Problem Solving, Equity, & Professionalism

> **CONNECT:** Use resources to enhance your skills as a supervisor.

People. Who can assist you in sharing samples of excellent planning strategies?

Books and Resources. Read *Active Learning: 101 Strategies* by Silberman (Allyn and Bacon).

Technology. Try www.ericir.syr.edu/virtual/lessons/ for ERIC Lesson Plans.

> **ACT:** Select the activities that will be useful to you or create your own.

ACTion #1. Share examples of effective planning with the student teacher.

ACTion #2. Discuss how to adapt and change lessons to meet the needs of students.

ACTion #3. Describe the differences in long planning versus plan book planning.

REFLECT: **Think about your role as a supervisor and write a one-page reflection.**

Choose to respond to the key questions on the previous page, create a prompt of your own, or answer the following question: How do I relate good planning to classroom management, assessment, and student learning?

What Does the Student Teacher Need to Think about Before Beginning?

1. Why am I teaching this lesson?

   - Required curriculum?

   - Student interest in topic?

   - My interest in topic?

2. What do I hope to accomplish?

   - Skill to be developed?

   - Concept to be discussed for understanding?

   - Product to be produced?

3. Who are the students?

   - Range of abilities?

   - Range of ages?

   - Ethnic diversity and varying cultures?

4. What is the time frame for teaching this lesson?

   - Part of a unit?

   - One period or block schedule?

   - Isolated lesson?

5. How will I begin the lesson to capture student attention?

   - Story or anecdote?

   - Relevance to their lives?

   - Props or visual displays?

6. Will I need other resources to teach this lesson?

   - Audiovisual or technology?

   - Student handouts?

   - Manipulative or visual displays?

7. How will students spend their time during the lesson?

   - Small group discussions? Individual? Large group?

   - Hands-on activity or experiment?

- Taking notes or observing?

8. How will this lesson be assessed?

   - Formal? Quiz or test?

   - Informal? Observation of learning?

   - Open-ended questions? Written? Verbal?

9. How will I close the lesson or close the class period?

   - Review and summary?

   - Collecting papers giving next assignments?

   - Allowing time for homework or questions?

10. Will there be homework or enrichment activities offered?

    - How will I collect later? Is it required or extra?

    - Will it count? What is the cooperating teacher's policy?

    - How will I grade it?

11. How will I know if I succeeded in teaching the lesson?

    - Self-assessment?

    - Response of students?

    - Cooperating teacher input?

12. How will the next lesson relate or build on this one?

Teachers and Planning

Share the types of planning you do with your student teacher.

1. Long Range: Yearly Planning and Term Planning

- How were plans created?
- What guides the plans?

  City/school system

  School or state curriculum guides

  Department
- What does the plan look like?

Short-term planning supports the goals of the long-term plans and puts into "action" these goals on a daily basis.

2. Short Term: Unit Planning

Units may be organized around themes or subjects areas. Some units are interdisciplinary and use a variety of knowledge content areas.

3. Short Term: Weekly Plan Book Planning

Share your plan book with the student teacher.

4. Short Term: Daily Lesson Plans

Daily lesson plans stem from long-range planning and short-term planning goals. Examples of daily lesson formats are located in this chapter.

What is the value to the daily plan in the scheme of long- and short-term planning?

Time and Planning

One of the biggest concerns of teachers is that there just is not enough time in the day to do all there is to do. The majority of the time spent should be on the curriculum that you have planned—not in making announcements, collecting lunch money, passing out materials, getting students into groups, or cleaning up. However, these tasks do need to get done!

A class period is your *allocated teaching time,* but it also needs to include housekeeping activities. *Instructional time* is the time when students are actually engaged in learning activities. Your lesson plan is the way to organize your thinking so that most of the allocated time is spent engaging students in learning and checking for understanding.

Use the following as a guide and include time *as a factor in designing lesson plans with your student teacher.*

ALLOCATED CLASS TIME: HOW MUCH SHOULD YOU SPEND?

Time _____ 1. Start of Class Period: Housekeeping Activities

- Required tasks

- Collection of homework

Time _____ 2. Beginning Lesson: Introducing or Connecting to Previous Day

- Motivation/relevance

- Overview

- Directions

- Purpose of lesson

Time _____ 3. Middle of Lesson

- Objective

- Key questions

- Students engaged in learning

- Activity

- Knowledge

- Student sharing

- Informal assessment and checking for understanding

73

Time _____   4. Closing of Lesson

  • Wrap-up

  • Review key points

  • Collection of materials/papers

Time _____   5. End of Class Period: Housekeeping Activities

  • Required tasks

  • Collection of classwork

Writing Teaching Objectives for Effective Lessons

Objectives state what the teacher wants the students to accomplish upon completion of the lesson. Students should be clear about objectives before they begin the lesson so that they know what is expected of them.

Lesson plan objectives should use verbs and be writen as one sentence. Bloom's Taxonomy organizes the verbs by levels of understanding, beginning with basic knowledge and moving up through comprehension, application, analysis, synthesis, and evaluation. Higher-level thinking is expected for verbs at levels 5 and 6. These verbs indicate *what the student should be doing.*

As your student teacher writes lesson plan objectives, guide him or her in selecting a verb and stating what is to be accomplished. Encourage him or her to vary the levels of complexity in the lessons—for example:

Name the planets, in order, beginning with the Sun.

Predict the ending of this story.

Explain the reasons for the start of the Civil War.

Bloom's Taxonomy	*Sample of Verbs to Use in Objectives*
6. Evaluation	choose, conclude, evaluate, defend, rank, support, rate, etc.
5. Synthesis	construct, create, formulate, revise, write, plan, predict, etc.
4. Analysis	analyze, classify, compare, contrast, debate, categorize, etc.
3. Application	apply, demonstrate, draw, show, solve, illustrate, etc.
2. Comprehension	describe, explain, paraphrase, summarize, rewrite, etc.
1. Knowledge	define, identify, list, memorize, spell, name, etc.

What do you, in the role of the cooperating teacher, need to do *to have your student teacher demonstrate a variety of learning objectives at all levels?*

Remember: An effective student teacher teaches so students meet the objectives stated in the lesson plan.

Creating a Plan from the Cooperating Teacher's Ideas

At the beginning of the student teaching experience, you might suggest to the student teacher that he or she teach part of a class or continue with a plan you may have already started. The following suggestions will guide your student teacher:

- Review the questions from What Does the Student Teacher Need to Think about Before Beginning? page in this chapter.

- Select a planning form from this chapter that meets the needs of the lesson.

- Copy the plan format (perhaps several copies in case you need to revise).

- Handwrite your objectives and procedures (pencil is best so you can erase and revise).

- Review the plan and check for accuracy and how much time it will take.

- Show the plan to your cooperating teacher *before* you teach the lesson.

- Revise the plan to include any suggestions made by your cooperating teacher.

- Teach the lesson.

- Self-assess: How did the plan work?

- Ask your cooperating teacher for feedback: What is the cooperating teacher's response to the lesson?

- Record suggestions and attach them to the plan. File this in your student teaching binder for future reference.

Daily Lesson Plan Model

Time of Class: <u>Period or time</u>   **Length of Period:** <u>How much time to teach</u>

Subject: <u>Content</u>

Date: <u>day you teach lesson</u>

Lesson Plan Title: <u>Write the name of the topic or class here</u>

Purpose: <u>Why are you teaching this lesson? What is the goal you are seeking to reach?</u>

Objectives: <u>Bloom's Taxonomy using verb—what the student will achieve or accomplish</u>

Theme or Unit # ___: <u>Is this an isolated lesson or part of a bigger curriculum unit? Number it as to where it fits in the sequence. If there is an expectation that students need prior knowledge to complete the lesson, how will you handle this with new students or those who have missed previous lessons?</u>

Key Questions: <u>What questions will you introduce to the students to guide the discussion and activities of the lesson? They should be broadly designed to encourage discussion and critical thinking. (Questions should not be designed with a yes or no answer.)</u>

Procedure: Note that the class period includes other housekeeping activities, such as collecting papers from the night before, announcing future school activities, collecting lunch money, and so on. These need to be incorporated into the lesson plan to avoid running out of teaching time.

Classroom Management Notes: Effective planning assures efficient teaching with a minimum of classroom discipline issues. Note what problems you may encounter as you implement this lesson. For example, if you are using many supplies and students need to leave their seats, you need to be prepared to supervise this to avoid problems.

Assessment Tool: What are you planning to use to check for understanding? List it here. Does it need to be collected?

Follow-Up: List any ending details that need to be put on the board or announced at the end of class, such as homework assignments, extra-credit options, or enrichment activities.

Student Teacher Self-Assessment: Write your impression of the lesson and what you would do differently next time you teach it. Write this response on the back of the lesson plan.

Sample Procedure for Use of Allotted Classroom Time

Time	Classroom Lesson	Teacher Behaviors: What Will You Be Doing?	Expected Student Behaviors: What Will the Students Be Doing?
5%	Starting class period	Housekeeping	Listening Passing in homework
10%	Beginning lesson	Introducing objectives, vocabulary, and key questions	Showing interest Participating, listening
70%	Middle of lesson	Facilitating a variety of activities for student learning	Collaborating Thinking, discussing Responding to key questions
10%	Closing lesson	Summarizing and reviewing lesson and setting goals for next lesson	Answering key questions Self-assessing
5%	Ending class period	Housekeeping	Passing in materials

Sample Plan

Time of Class: _____ **Length of Period:** _____ **Subject:** _____

Date: _____

Lesson Plan Title: _____

Purpose: _____

Objective(s): _____

Theme or Unit Number: _____

Key Questions:

1. _____

2. _____

3. _____

Procedure

Time	Classroom Period	Teacher Behaviors: What Will You Be Doing?	Expected Student Behaviors: What Will the Students Be Doing?
	Starting class period	Housekeeping	
	Beginning lesson	Motivation/Key Questions	
	Middle of lesson	Activities	

Time	Classroom Period	Teacher Behaviors: What Will You Be Doing?	Expected Student Behaviors: What Will the Students Be Doing?
	Closing lesson	Review	
	Ending class period	Housekeeping	

Classroom Management Notes: _____

Assessment Tool: _____

Follow-Up: _____

Student Teacher Self-Assessment: on back or attached

Sample Lesson Plan: Early Childhood

Date: _____

Subject: _____

Unit Lesson #: _____

Objectives for Lesson:
1. _____
2. _____

Skills	Materials	Assessment
		What will all students learn? What will most students learn? What will some students learn?

Developmental Procedure for Lesson:
1.
2.
3.

Notes/Modifications:

Sample Lesson Plan: Elementary/Middle School

Date: _____

Subject: _____

Lesson # _____ of Unit _____

Objectives:

1. _____

2. _____

3. _____

Key Vocabulary:		**Key Questions:**
1. _____ 4. _____		1. _____
2. _____ 5. _____		2. _____
3. _____ 6. _____		3. _____

Materials/Resources/Technology:

Procedure (Beginning, Middle, Closing):

Assessment:

Classroom Management Notes/Lesson Modifications:

Homework/Follow-Up/Enrichment:

Teacher Self-Assessment of Lesson (What would you do differently? Write on back or attach.)

Sample Lesson Plan: Secondary School

Date: _____

Period: _____ Time: _____ Block: _____

Subject: _____

Objectives:	Key Questions:
1. _____	1. _____
_____	_____
2. _____	2. _____
_____	_____
3. _____	3. _____
_____	_____

Vocabulary:

_____   _____   _____

_____   _____   _____

_____   _____   _____

Textbook: _____ Pages: _____ Material/Handouts: _____

Procedure

Introduction	Overview:
Mini-Lecture	Key Points:
Students Pairs, Group Work, or Way in Which Students Are Engaged	Activities:
Closing	Summary:

Assessment:

Homework:

General Guidelines for Designing a Unit

A unit is an organized group of lesson plans with a beginning, various activities, and a culmination. The unit may be subject based, interdisciplinary, or thematic. It can last as long as a semester or as short as a week. It has overarching themes and concepts to be learned through daily lessons. Teachers typically organize their teaching in *teaching units* by skills for early childhood, by *subjects or themes* for elementary/middle, and by *subject-area topics* at secondary levels. Units are organized around books students have read, historical wars, science themes, topics, or anything you can think of that relates to knowledge.

A unit will have a general outline or plan for implementation; the daily lesson plans demonstrate in detail how the unit is implemented in the classroom. Lesson plans are created as you move through the unit, rather than ahead of time, since there are often changes from the original plan.

QUESTIONS TO CONSIDER BEFORE BEGINNING A UNIT

- What is the purpose of the unit?

- How much time will the unit need? How many lessons?

- What do students already know?

- What would students like to learn or know?

- How will the unit be introduced?

- What are the key questions that need to be answered?

- Is prior knowledge necessary?

- Will the unit have a theme?

- Will the unit cross disciplines? Is team teaching involved?

- Will any special activities be part of the unit?

- Will I need special materials or audiovisuals for this unit?

- Will guest speakers or field trips be part of the unit?

Check your university models for units and review units you have learned about in methods courses. How will you organize your unit for student teaching? What would you like to include for lesson activities in your unit?

Unit Organizers

Unit organizers are valuable ways to map out your unit. Ask the cooperating teacher and university supervisor to share examples of unit organizers with you that can serve as models for your unit outline.

Title of Unit

Purpose	*Objectives*	*Key Questions*	*Key Vocabulary*	*Materials*
Assessments	*Possible Daily Lesson Activities*	*Opening Activity*	*Culmination*	*Guests or Trips*

Another way to organize a unit is using a web. Adapt this example to web your unit.

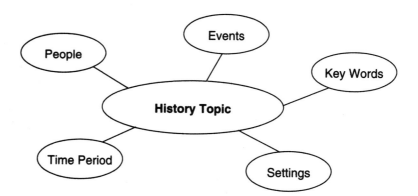

Planing for Understanding

A teacher knows he or she has a good plan when, at the end of the lesson or unit, there is evidence of student understanding or skill development. An effective teacher, like an architect, designs a plan that will create a solid foundation for creative and original thinking. Teachers present information not to just be memorized for the weekly test, but to be understood and integrated into a student's thinking. This is not an easy task, but it is one that should be kept in your mind as you begin to plan lessons. What do you want students to know, understand, and be able to do as a result of your lesson?

FIVE STEPS TO SUCCESSFUL LESSON PLANNING

1. **Think about breadth or depth** as you design your lessons and units.

   - Are you aiming for breadth in your lessons (i.e., connecting this concept to other concepts or relevant experiences)?

     Students explain why or why not

     Students extend the concept to others

     Students think about and give examples of similar concepts

   - Are you aiming for depth in your lessons (i.e., looking more at the detail about this idea)?

     Students question the information

     Students analyze the facts

     Students prove something

2. **Set priorities** for assessing student growth in lessons and units.

   - What do you expect all students to be familiar with or know?

     Be able to do in this class?

     To really understand for lasting learning?

3. **Select measurement tools** to determine student understanding.

   - How will you know students understand?

     What do *all* students have to know? How will you know?

What do *most* students have to know? How will you know?

What will *some* students know? How will you know?

4. **Create meaningful learning experiences** that engage and support learning (not just busywork).

   • Motivate: Have you included a "hook" to gain attention and provide relevance?

   • Questions: Do you have key questions that promote discussion and thinking?

   • Practice: Do you have time for students to practice and engage in activity?

   • Self-Assessment: Do you allow students time to reflect on their work and set goals?

5. **Observe what you are doing** during a class period.

If Teacher Does This...	*Students Respond This Way...*
Lectures and talks from front of class	Give short answers, take notes, listen
Promotes cooperative learning Inquiry Seminar circles Discussion Open-ended questions	Collaborate in groups or pairs, question, revise, brainstorm, construct meaning

What are other ways in which you can assess your lesson planning skills?

How Do You Know When to "Let Go"?

As a teacher, your primary responsibility is the students in your classroom. When you invite a beginner into your space, you take a risk. Will the student teacher be able to work with you? Will the student teacher be able to teach the classes and keep you on schedule? Some student teachers are more gifted than others. Some need more time to move through the stages of development. With your guidance and nonjudgmental feedback, your student teacher will likely achieve success. Use this chart to guide your decisions in moving your student teacher through the stages of development.

Stage 1	Observing	Student teacher observes cooperating teacher.	Beginning weeks of the practicum, formally and informally throughout
Stage 2	Assisting	Student teacher and cooperating teacher coteach while sharing responsibilities.	Beginning and middle weeks of the practicum
Stage 3	Full responsibility	Student teacher takes over for an agreed-upon period of time. Cooperating teacher observes student teacher.	Toward the end of the practicum experience

Your feedback to the student teacher will guide the student through these three stages of development. How will you decide when it is time to "let go"?

Cooperating Teacher's Reflection

JOURNAL ENTRY

How do you feel about the lesson planning process with your student teacher?

Date: _____

_____

_____

_____

_____

_____

REFLECTIVE QUESTIONS

1. What have you learned about your own planning process?

_____

2. How important do you think planning is?

_____

3. What would you do differently next time you share planning with a student teacher?

_____

4. What really worked this time?

_____

Final Reminders and Helpful Hints

_____ Student teachers should realize that plans are not cut in stone and that it is permissible to change a plan during a lesson if there is a teachable moment to capture, or if the students are not responding. The important thing is to know why they changed their plan and what they would do differently next time.

_____ Review the plans for teacher talking time (TTT) to ensure that students will have a chance to participate! Some student teachers do all the talking in a period.

_____ Talk to the student teacher about various abilities of students and how a plan might be modified to meet the needs of this diverse population.

_____ Pacing a lesson is a critical part of planning. Too much to do in a lesson plan or too little activity can create problems. Talk about pacing a lesson with your student teacher.

_____ There may be problems with planning—allow your student teacher to make some errors and to learn by doing. However, major problems that you might see in a plan can be avoided under your careful guidance. Have the student teacher focus on how students are engaged during a lesson.

_____ Talk about what to do if some students in the class finish the assigned task earlier than others—should this be part of the lesson plan?

_____ Do not let lesson planning become overwhelming paperwork for the student teacher!

_____ Model good plans by sharing some of yours.

_____ As student teachers pick up a new subject, they may move from a long form plan to the block plan to avoid too much paperwork.

_____   List your own hints here:

_____   _____

_____   _____

_____   _____

_____   _____

_____   _____

CHAPTER 6

Using a Variety of Teaching Strategies

What we think, or what we know, or what we believe, is, in the end, of little consequence. The only consequence is what we do.

John Rushin

There are many approaches, interpretations, methods, and strategies currently being used in classrooms. Most student teachers should be prepared to apply the methods they have learned in their strategies classes. This chapter highlights a variety of approaches and can be used as a reminder to you that the student teacher should not just mimic your style but rather use this opportunity to practice a variety of methods. The next chapter will highlight ways to make the delivery of the plan and strategies successful.

Lesson plans work only when appropriate strategies and delivery techniques are used. Some student teachers have outstanding plans and good intentions but lack the ability to select a method that will enhance the plan and create an opportunity for student learning.

The methods discussed in this chapter serve only as a sample of the types of many strategies the student teacher might use during the practicum. The student teacher should be able to see that different methods may produce different student interactions and end results. Lesson objectives can be met in a variety of ways, and the student teacher should be encouraged to develop a number of different strategies.

The checklists, forms, and samples in this chapter will give you an overview of current strategies so that you can coach your student teacher to use many techniques.

Lesson Plan

Time: First few weeks

Title: Teaching Strategies

Purpose: To review current strategies with the student teacher to ensure use during the practicum

Objectives:
- To demonstrate methods before asking the student teacher to teach them
- To allow the student teacher to begin by selecting those methods with which he or she is most comfortable
- To encourage the use of many different methods

Materials: Forms in this chapter

Procedure:
1. Review with the student teacher his or her knowledge of methods and add to the list provided.
2. Demonstrate several methods for the student teacher as appropriate.
3. Coach the student teacher through a new method.
4. Discuss why a variety of methods is useful.
5. Review methods seen during observations.

Other Thoughts/ Notes: The student teacher may want to go through college notes from methods courses and select some of those ideas to try at this time.

University Supervisor Suggestions

PLAN: **Organize your thoughts and materials, and prepare for your role.**

Key Questions

1. Which strategies will the student teacher be expected to demonstrate to meet the needs of the diverse learners in his or her classroom?

2. How will the student teacher document the strategies used?

Teaching Competency Focus Areas for Chapter 6

Knowledge, Communication, **Instructional Practice**, Evaluation, **Problem Solving, Equity,** & Professionalism

CONNECT: **Use resources to enhance your skills as a supervisor.**

People. Are there models of effective strategies for the student teacher to view?

Books and Resources. Review the multiple intelligences literature.

Technology. Try www.ericir.syr.edu/virtual/lessons/ for ERIC Lesson Plans.

ACT: **Select the activities that will be useful to you or create your own.**

ACTion #1. Make a list of the strategies you will be expecting the student to use.

ACTion #2. Inventory what the student teacher is already able to do.

ACTion #3. Discuss the strategies and why some work for some student teachers but not for others.

> **REFLECT:** **Think about your role as a supervisor and write a one-page reflection.**

Choose to respond to the key questions on the previous page, create a prompt of your own, or answer the following question: What do I want the student teacher to really understand about using a variety of teaching strategies?

Using Instructional Materials to Enhance Teaching and Learning

Textbooks are often used as the basic curriculum for a classroom; however, they do not have to be the *only* resource that is used. Ask your cooperating teacher to share his or her opinion about the textbooks you will be using this semester. Review all the materials and teacher's editions that are part of the textbook series. How does the textbook relate to your school curriculum?

Audiovisual materials and computers can be an integral component in creating a rich teaching and learning environment. They also provide other ways for students with varied learning styles to approach a learning activity.

Review the following list of materials and code them by your level of familiarity (C = comfortable with using this resource, N = need to learn how to use this resource).

C or N	Audiovisual and Technology	Where I Might Integrate into My Teaching This Semester
	Overhead projector	
	Computer	
	CD	
	VCR and TV	
	Video camera	
	Tape recorder with headsets	
	Slide projector	
	Filmstrip projector	
	Video recorder	
	Instructional Equipment	
	Copy machine	
	Transparencies	

C or N	Audiovisual and Technology	Where I Might Integrate into My Teaching This Semester
	Instructional Aids	
	Prop/Maps/Globes	
	Calculators, geoboards, tangrams, and other manipulatives	
	Science experiment materials	

Process Approaches to Learning

Cooperative learning, process writing, and hands-on math and science are some of the ways in which teachers are being encouraged to teach. If you, as a cooperating teacher, are not familiar with these methods and are unable to demonstrate them, you should seek out a teacher in the building who can share the methods with you and your student teacher.

Some process approaches lend themselves better to one subject than to another, but all subjects can surely be matched to some type of process-related activity. Think of specific ways in which you and your student teacher can design lessons that use process approaches. Here are some examples:

Process	Subject	Activity
Cooperative learning	History	Make a mural as a team.
Process writing	Language	With a partner, write a story and edit each other's work.
Hands-on	Math	Independently use a calculator to compute problems.
Hands-on	Science	In triads, build a boat that will float the longest.

Other process activities may include role-plays, debates, plays, mimes, creative dramatics, puppet shows, and other presentations.

Using Textbooks

The textbook is often the tool used with the whole class, but it does not have to be the only resource used; in fact, there is a danger in relying on the textbook too much. However, it is important for student teachers to know how to use the teacher's manual and when to use the textbook. This is important because the text is a valuable resource full of rich ideas. It is just not to be relied on as the *whole* curriculum. Overuse of the textbook can lead to less engaging lessons and possible discipline problems. Do the following with your student teacher:

_____ Review the textbooks and manuals.

_____ Review any other resource/enrichment material that supports the textbook.

_____ Try to get the student teacher his or her own teacher's manual.

_____ Encourage the student teacher to read the teacher's edition and student information *before* teaching a lesson using the textbook.

_____ Note in the lessons how often the textbook is used and if it is appropriate.

_____ Note if textbook use is always within a large-group, teacher-directed lesson. If so, assist the student teacher in creating other alternatives to use the text (e.g., two students reading the text to each other, small groups with one student reading, etc.).

_____ Ask if the student teacher has questions about using textbooks and what his or her experience is in using textbooks.

_____ Explain the differences between textbook styles.

_____ Explain textbook use as it relates to the school curriculum.

_____ Create a variety of interesting ways to use the textbook in the classroom.

_____

_____

Effectively Teaching the Whole Class

Large-group instruction is a common practice in many schools and can be an effective strategy if it is used along with a variety of other approaches, props, and techniques. When speaking to the whole class, there are several ways to create active participation on the part of the students. Lecturing is not the most exciting way to present material, yet many teachers do it. Encourage your student teacher to engage the students if the whole-group instruction or lecture method is going to be used.

Any of these suggestions for whole-group instruction or presentations by the teacher can be adapted to work in smaller groups or partners for part of the class:

_____ 1. Divide the presentation into three parts: (a) The introduction, with a strong motivating set of facts or personal story from the teacher, "hooks" the students into listening and clarifies the purpose of the lesson; (b) the middle part should be the heart of the lesson, with skills, demonstrations with props, or information giving; and (c) the conclusion should include some review of main points and time for questions.

_____ 2. Before the presentation, give each student an index card with a word or phrase on it that you will use during the lesson. When the student hears it, he or she writes on the index card what he or she thinks it means and the time it was mentioned. At the end of the presentation, students can share the new words they learned in context during the lesson.

_____ 3. If the whole-group lesson involves viewing a video, slide show, or filmstrip, have the students try to find a certain number of items or listen for certain facts (like a visual scavenger hunt). At the end, see how many students found things and share.

_____ 4. Before the presentation or video, ask the students what they would like to know at the end of the class. List all the questions on the board, weave the answers into the presentation, and at the end, see how many students heard the answers.

_____ 5. List an idea of your own here:

_____

_____

Using Questions for Higher-Level Thinking

It is important to encourage the student teacher to monitor the number and kinds of questions asked during a lesson. Beginning teachers often ask more questions during a class period than could possibly be answered and spend much of their energy answering their own questions. An easy way for the student teacher to check questions is to audiotape a lesson and listen to it later. You may want to have the student teacher tape you teaching a lesson and listen to the tape together and code the questions by thinking levels.

Using Bloom's Taxonomy as a guide, questions can be rated from rote memory responses to high-level evaluative questions. A classroom presentation should be rich in a variety of types of questions asked by both students and the teacher. With older students, you can teach them the types of questions and let them tell you what you are asking.

1. Ask the student teacher to note the number, frequency, and timing of questions during a lesson you teach and a lesson he or she teaches.

2. Ask the student teacher to listen for different types of questions and to note the number of questions at each level and write it on the line in front of the level of the question.

    _____ first   *Knowledge:* rote memory, recall

    _____ second   *Comprehension:* asks for some understanding

    _____ third   *Application:* Must be able to apply the information

    _____ fourth   *Analysis:* Take a whole and break into parts

    _____ fifth   *Synthesis*: Take parts and make a whole

    _____ sixth   *Evaluation:* most complex, needs to use many skills to solve

3. Ask the student teacher to note how long he or she "waits" for a student response to a question. Harder questions will take a longer time to think through. Discuss results of this.

Modifying Lessons for Students with Special Needs

Students with academic special needs often have varying abilities. Be sure to explain all the ways you modify lessons to meet the needs of the diverse learners in your classroom.

EXAMPLES OF MODIFICATIONS

- Giving a student more time to complete an assignment
- Assigning fewer questions or examples to be completed
- Allowing a student to tape record his or her answers instead of writing
- Working with a partner who would write the answers the students stated verbally
- Accepting printed work instead of cursive
- Using the computer to complete work
- Other _____

SHARE WITH YOUR STUDENT TEACHER

- How you know which activities you can leave incomplete and which have to be done
- How you pace a lesson so that all or most students complete the task
- How you create high expectations for learners who work more slowly

Discuss with your student teacher how lessons are currently being modified for individual students in your classroom. List the student and the modification in your lesson plan:

Student #1 _____ Modification _____

Student #2 _____ Modification _____

Student #3 _____ Modification _____

Student #4 _____ Modification _____

Student #5 _____ Modification _____

Cooperating Teacher's Reflection

How effective was your demonstration of a variety of teaching strategies with your student teacher?

JOURNAL ENTRY

Date: _____

_____

_____

_____

_____

_____

_____

REFLECTIVE QUESTIONS

1. How many of these strategies do you regularly use as a teacher? List.

_____

_____

2. Which methods are you most comfortable with and why?

_____

_____

3. How has sharing this information helped you as a teacher?

_____

_____

Final Reminders and Helpful Hints

_____ Encourage the student teacher to use many approaches, but remember that the student teacher will not be able to master them all at once! Be patient—select one or more for mastery and use the others to build on the student's variety of skills.

_____ Remember to demonstrate any strategy you expect the student teacher to use before he or she tries it with students in the room. There should be an observation and a discussion about the technique to avoid possible pitfalls. What you see as a commonsense situation to avoid may not be the case with the student teacher.

_____ Discuss the role of effective classroom-management techniques, especially as related to process and group activities.

_____ Review the role of "practice" in the lesson as part of learning new skills. For example, in math, students may be asked to write word problems or facts. How does this relate to the lesson and the objectives designed in the plan? Make sure student teachers understand the difference between practice work and busywork.

_____ Write your hints for using methods:

_____

_____

_____

_____

_____

_____

_____

_____

CHAPTER 7

Facilitating Learning

Go confidently in the direction of your dreams.
Henry David Thoreau

How to present a lesson is perhaps the most important skill a student teacher has to develop during the practicum. Some student teachers have a natural presentation style, and others are quite nervous about appearing before a group of students. Enthusiasm and personal sharing are vital to motivating students in a classroom. Discuss this with your student teacher. A student teacher does not just "impart" information to the students in the class; he or she must also facilitate learning.

The student teacher's voice and manner directly influence the success of the lesson. The most well-written lesson plan and the most appropriate strategy will not be effective if they are delivered in a half-hearted, unenthusiastic manner. Teachers often have to be performers to gain attention and to excite the students. Putting forward an alive presentation is critical to achieving success with students in the classroom.

We as teachers often do things unconsciously and have difficulty explaining how we actually gain student attention. The purpose of this chapter is not to have the student teacher copy your teaching style, but to have the student teacher develop a personal style of his or her own. How you facilitate learning and present information in the classroom will vary from the presentation of other teachers. Allow the student teacher to talk with other teachers to learn more about various presentation styles and how the teachers in your school actually encourage students to want to learn.

The forms, samples, and checklists in this chapter will remind you of the specific aspects of presenting a lesson and encourage you to coach your student teacher in discovering his or her own presentation style.

Lesson Plan

Time: As lessons are taught

Title: Presentation and Teaching Style

Purpose: To encourage and demonstrate successful strategies for lesson presentation

Objectives:
- To brainstorm techniques for delivery
- To demonstrate several ways to present lessons
- To think about what good delivery means

Materials: Forms in this handbook

Procedure:
1. Discuss the importance of delivery with the student teacher.
2. Allow the student teacher to observe several teachers and compare styles.
3. Allow the student teacher to try delivery techniques.
4. Reflect on your experiences.

Other Thoughts/ Notes: Delivery and presentation style can make or break a lesson plan. It is an integral part of classroom-management skills. Getting the attention of the students is critical to teaching!

University Supervisor Suggestions

PLAN: Organize your thoughts and materials, and prepare for your role.

Key Questions

1. How does the student teacher's presentation affect the learning outcome?

2. How do speaking and movement by the teacher relate to teaching?

Teaching Competency Focus Areas for Chapter 7

Knowledge, Communication, Instructional Practice, Evaluation, Problem Solving, Equity, & Professionalism

CONNECT: Use resources to enhance your skills as a supervisor.

People. Encourage the student teacher to visit a variety of classrooms to observe presentation.

Books and Resources. Encourage the student teacher to view Association for Supervision and Curriculum Development (ASCD) videotapes of good teachers.

Technology. For current national information, contact the National Education Association (NEA): www.nea.org/cet

ACT: Select the activities that will be useful to you or create your own.

ACTion #1. Model effective presentation skills for the student teacher.

ACTion #2. Observe the student teacher and highlight his or her strengths in these areas.

ACTion #3. Discuss with the student teacher how to create environments for listening.

> **REFLECT:** **Think about your role as a supervisor and write a one-page reflection.**

Choose to respond to the key questions on the previous page, create a prompt of your own, or answer the following question: How can I, as a supervisor, assist the student teacher who is having difficulty giving directions to his or her students?

Important Aspects of Presenting a Lesson

1. Look at your own lesson delivery for one day and jot down all the things you think contributed to successful delivery.

   _____

   _____

   _____

2. Talk with three of your colleagues and ask them how they successfully present a lesson to a class. Ask for information that relates to giving directions, how much time they talk, how they use their voices, their movement in the classroom, and any other aspects of presentation.

   _____

   _____

   _____

3. Think about the pitfalls in the delivery of a lesson. What are the danger signals?

   _____

   _____

   _____

4. How will you share the pitfalls with a student teacher? How can you assist a student teacher in seeing those danger signals?

   _____

   _____

   _____

Speaking Skills

Every teacher has a unique manner and personality. Voice is a major part of this manner. Some personalities lend themselves to more enthusiastic presentation than do others. The student teacher may want to audiotape a lesson and answer these questions, or you may use it as a form of feedback.

USING YOUR VOICE IN THE CLASSROOM

1. **Volume:** What is the volume of the student teacher's voice at the beginning of the lesson, during the lesson, and at the closing of the lesson?

   _____

   _____

2. **Pronunciation:** Does the student teacher pronounce words correctly? Does he or she use words that relate to the content of the lesson and the age of the students?

   _____

   _____

3. **Articulation:** How clearly does the student teacher express himself or herself?

   _____

   _____

4. **Speed:** What is the rate of speaking during the lesson? Is it too fast or too slow?

   _____

   _____

5. How was voice used to reprimand or praise?

_____

_____

6. How much time did the student teacher spend talking, as opposed to engaging the students in the classroom?

_____

_____

Giving Directions

How do you give directions to your classes? Share your specific strategies for presenting information to your students so that all students understand what they are supposed to be doing. How do you know what kind of directions your students need? Notice how you prefer to receive directions when you are learning something new. Ask your student teacher to observe you as you give directions and to share his or her observations with you.

1. How do you give directions?

   - *Verbal:* Are they clear? How long does it take to give them? Are there several steps?

   - *Visual:* Are they written on the board, overhead, or given to students?

2. What does your voice sound like when giving directions?

   - *Volume:* Can the directions be heard at the back of the room?

   - *Pronunciation:* Are the words pronounced correctly?

   - *Articulation:* How clearly are words expressed?

   - *Speed:* Are key points spoken slowly enough for all to understand?

3. Where are you standing in the classroom when giving directions?

   - *Position:* Where did the teacher stand? Was the teacher sitting?

   - *Movement:* Did the teacher move around to check on the students?

4. What else did the student teacher notice about your directions?

   - *Clarification:* Was there an opportunity for students to ask clarifying questions?

   - What else did you notice?

Ask the student teacher to think about:

1. How can complicated directions create problems for students who may be learning challenged?

2. What can you do to avoid potential problems related to poor directions?

Movement in the Classroom

Use these questions as a basis for a discussion. Share with your student teacher and ask the student teacher to observe the ways you move in the classroom. Ask the student teacher to jot down any questions he or she has about how a teacher should move in the classroom.

1. How does movement in the classroom enhance the delivery of a lesson?

_____

_____

_____

2. What are effective movements in the classroom?

_____

_____

_____

3. Where should a teacher teach? How does it depend on the type of lesson?

_____

_____

_____

4. How often should a teacher move during a lesson?

_____

_____

Cooperating Teacher's Reflection

How has thinking about delivering a lesson helped you as a teacher?

JOURNAL ENTRY

Date: _____

_____

_____

_____

_____

_____

_____

REFLECTIVE QUESTIONS

1. What helpful hints can you share with the student teacher about voice and movement? How will you demonstrate these skills?

_____

_____

2. What will you do if you see an inappropriate behavior in your student teacher related to voice, direction giving, or movement?

_____

_____

3. How will you assist your student teacher when his or her personality style interferes with the lesson presentation or facilitation of learning?

_____

_____

Final Reminders and Helpful Hints

_____ Encourage the student teacher to try a variety of styles and presentation techniques.

_____ Don't ask the student teacher to do things you are not comfortable doing or have not demonstrated.

_____ Be sensitive to personality traits when asking a student teacher to change some aspect in delivery.

_____ Encourage audiotaping first so the student teacher can hear his or her own voice. When the student teacher has some level of confidence, move to videotaping.

_____ Remember that the student teacher's state of mind, self-esteem, stability, and trust levels are all preconditions for establishing and facilitating learning in the classroom.

_____ Write your reminders here:

_____

_____

_____

_____

_____

_____

_____

_____

_____

_____

CHAPTER 8

Supervision Techniques

Allow your student teacher to try new things and risk failure. Be willing to let the student teacher experiment.

Amy Vena

The purpose of this chapter is to give you some techniques and suggestions for supervising your student teacher. Many student teachers feel their cooperating teachers do not give them regular feedback about specific aspects of their teaching. Cooperating teachers often feel uncomfortable giving any type of corrective feedback or just praising all the good aspects of the lesson. So, in many cases, no feedback at all is given, or minimal comments are made after a lesson.

Student teachers also need to feel comfortable in experimenting with their ideas. They should not be intimidated by supervisory techniques, nor should they see them as judgments on their teaching. Striving for "perfect lesson presentations" should not be the goal of the student teacher. Rather, he or she should be striving to create a learning environment for the students. Presenting information is one aspect of facilitating learning, but it should not be the only goal. When you supervise and give feedback, you need to be aware that you, as a coach, are also creating a learning environment for your student teacher. Encourage risk taking and new ideas. Your student teacher may never have another chance to have a teacher's input on his or her teaching.

The techniques in this chapter are designed to be nonjudgmental. They are based on clinical supervision and peer coaching models used by college supervisors, peer coaches, and mentors. *Nonjudgmental feedback* means you give the data (information) you observe during a lesson to the student teacher. You may want to ask the student teacher to share what he or she would like you to observe prior to the observation. This encourages the student teacher to discover ways to improve. The data would be given to the student teacher at a postconference (explained in Chapter 9).

The use of more formal supervision techniques is a way to replace the general comments cooperating teachers often make, such as, "That was a great lesson" or "The students weren't very good today." The techniques provide you with more concrete data that make you aware of the details of the lesson and provide student teachers with more specific information to guide their teaching.

The process can be very useful in assisting a student teacher's growth. The cooperating teacher becomes another set of eyes in the classroom, and the data collected during the lesson becomes a valuable way to review key components of a student teacher's teaching. It also provides an opportunity for you to grow as well, because any time you reflect on teaching, you will see things you do with the students.

A major advantage of using the techniques is that the student teacher is a willing partner who understands what is being observed. In fact, in many cases, as in peer coaching, the colleague being observed actually tells the observer what to look for during the lesson.

Before beginning any formal observation of the student teacher, share what you are doing and the forms you will be using. You may even want him or her to observe you using any of these techniques first to try out the model. Keep the anxiety level to a minimum. Create an environment that encourages collegial conversation and open communication.

It is important to set up ground rules for observation that both of you understand. Discuss how this information will be used. Specific observations throughout the practicum are valuable experiences for you and the student teacher in being able to judge progress. Planned observations should be more regular at the beginning of the semester and gradually be lessened as the practicum moves to the end. Some practitioners feel that leaving the room and letting the student teachers learn on their own is the best way to give them the *real* teaching experience. In many ways, this is true, but leaving the student teachers alone for long periods of time throughout the practicum and at the end may be a missed opportunity for cooperating teachers to guide their students.

Many student teachers do not always *see* what they need to know. Trial by fire alone in a classroom is a frustrating experience. Another pair of eyes through a formal observation system gives them nonjudgmental feedback and gives you concrete information you may need to refer to at a later date.

Some supervisors suggest that student teachers should be trained in the same clinical techniques as the cooperating teachers and should use them for observing during the first few weeks. If you feel this is appropriate, use the techniques in this chapter in conjunction with the guided observation suggestions given in Chapter 4.

Before you formally observe and collect data, set up a time for a preconference with your student teacher. At this time, review the form you will be using, have the student teacher share the lesson plan, and discuss the goals of the lesson.

The forms and checklists in this chapter will get you started toward an organized supervision of your student. Create techniques of your own or modify any of these to meet your needs.

Lesson Plan

Time: After the student teacher has taught

Title: Supervision Techniques for the Cooperating Teacher

Purpose: To provide the cooperating teacher with some easy strategies for collecting nonjudgmental data while a student teacher is teaching

Objectives:
- To think about what makes a good teacher
- To select appropriate supervision techniques
- To prepare a preconference
- To observe using one or more techniques
- To reflect on the experience

Procedure:
1. Discuss how you will observe in a preconference.
2. Do your observation and collect data.
3. Reflect on the experience.

Other Thoughts/ Notes: The focus of the observation should be in collecting nonjudgmental data so that the student teacher can start to see what is going on during the course of the lesson. Specific data are more useful than general comments. Let the student teacher make sense of the data before you make judgments about what happened.

University Supervisor Suggestions

> **PLAN:** Organize your thoughts and materials, and prepare for your role.

Key Questions

1. What are you looking for in the student teacher's teaching?

2. What are your expectations for the college requirements?

Teaching Competency Focus Areas for Chapter 8

Knowledge, Communication, Instructional Practice, **Evaluation,** Problem Solving, Equity, & Professionalism

> **CONNECT:** Use resources to enhance your skills as a supervisor.

People. Ask your supervisor for support and guidance as you begin this process.

Books and Resource. Look into clinical supervision as well as Harry K. Wong books and tapes.

Technology. Discover any sites for supervisors!

> **ACT:** Select the activities that will be useful to you or create your own.

ACTion #1. Discuss the supervision process with the student and the cooperating teacher.

ACTion #2. Learn and try several techniques for gathering data.

ACTion #3. Ask your students to audiotape several lessons and write reflections.

REFLECT: **Think about your role as a supervisor and write a one-page reflection.**

Choose to respond to the key questions on the previous page, create a prompt of your own, or answer the following question: How will I carry out my supervision responsibilities?

Roles and Responsibilites: Who Does What?

The Student Teaching Triad consists of the cooperating teacher, the student teacher, and the college supervisor. Each person plays a part in the development of a new teacher.

COLLEGE SUPERVISOR'S ROLE: "VISITING COACH"

- Responsible for providing overview of all requirements

- Responsible for providing support and guidance

- Responsible for giving feedback that promotes development

- Responsible for providing both formative and summative feedback in context of supervision

- Responsible for "close-out" meeting with student teacher to review all requirements

- Responsible for preparing student for certification check-out meeting

- Responsible for modeling profesional behavior

- Others: _____

_____

COOPERATING TEACHER'S DAILY ROLE AND RESPONSIBILITIES: "DAILY COACH"

(See effective cooperating teacher behaviors in Chapter 1.)

- Responsible for welcoming the student teacher

- Responsible for providing an environment for learning

- Responsible for working collaboratively with the college supervisor

- Responsible for offering suggestions and models for teaching

- Responsible for modeling professional behavior

- Others: _____

_____

STUDENT TEACHER'S ROLE: "PROSPECTIVE TEACHER"

- Responsible for completing all college requirements
- Responsible for attendance at school every day and making up any sick days
- Responsible for completing all certification requirements
- Responsible for 100 percent participation during practicum
- Responsible for accepting constructive feedback and implementing it
- Responsible for professionalism and confidentiality
- Others: _____

_____

What Are You Looking For? Observing Your Student Teacher

When observing your student teacher, you are looking for evidence that the student teacher is progressing as a beginning teacher and that he or she has the skills to maintain his or her own classroom independently. The ultimate goal is to document, through supervision, the basic teaching competencies. The student teacher will also have related college requirements to complete.

As a cooperating teacher, you should document teaching instruction through specific observable behaviors. Use the following chart to guide you as you learn to understand which behavior matches the teaching competencies and principles of teaching. Add new expected behaviors as you progress through the student teaching experience. You will note that the competencies and principles are very broad and often difficult to measure—that is why you should use specific behaviors to communicate your observations.

Teaching Behaviors That Relate to Required Teaching Competencies

Teaching Competencies	Teaching Principles	Example of Specific Classroom Behavior by Student Teacher
Knowledge of subject	Demonstrates a current working knowledge of the subject	Designs lesson and unit plans that are accurate and implements them with confidence
Communication	Communicates high expectations and high standards for all learners	Regularly discusses progress with students in the classroom and provides parent updates
Instructional practice	Effectively plans instruction and manages the daily and long-term environment for teaching	Daily, weekly, and monthly plans for student growth are completed and adapted as needed Classroom is orderly and shows an understanding of child growth and development

Teaching Competencies	Teaching Principles	Example of Specific Classroom Behavior by Student Teacher
Evaluation	Determines appropriate standards for all learners and incorporates time for individual differences using both formal and informal assessments Uses an inquiry approach to looking at teaching and looking through self-assessment	Designs teacher-made tests that are challenging and that match the objective of the lesson plan taught Uses other assessments appropriately and adapts for learners where needed Maintains a journal and thinks about the real issues in a classroom and talks with others about them in critical conversations
Problem Solving	Demonstrates an understanding and openness to student challenges while fostering students' critical and creative thinking in the classroom	Designs lessons to stimulate and promote critical thinking and student questions using a wide variety of teaching strategies and inquiry approaches
Equity	Addresses and appreciates the diversity of students in the classroom	Uses teaching strategies and lessons that include all students from other cultures, genders, and special needs, and promotes integrated heterogeneous groups
Professionalism	Demonstrates professionalism through collaboration and participation in all aspects of school	Reads current journals, completes all requirements on time, attends in-service workshops with cooperating teacher, and participates fully as a professional during student teaching

Selecting Observation Techniques

Talk with the student teacher and supervisor to decide how many times during the semester you want to formally preconference and collect data. Check the techniques you would like to try and write the Day/Time/Lesson you intend to observe when you try the technique for the first time.

_____ **Scripting.** (Writing everything you notice during the lesson; a profile of the lesson in narrative form)

Observation Day/Time/Lesson: _____

_____ **Verbal Feedback.** (Listening to the student teacher's speaking as it relates to asking questions, giving praise, talk time, reprimanding, or gender)

Observation Day/Time/Lesson: _____

_____ **Movement.** (Recording how the teacher moves around the room or how students interact with teacher, or both)

Observation Day/Time/Lesson: _____

_____ **Timing.** (Recording time it takes for introduction, giving directions, answering questions, doing assignments, cleaning up, etc.)

Observation Day/Time/Lesson: _____

_____ **Audiotaping.** (Providing equipment and taping the student teacher for voice, articulation, directions, or any specific aspect of speech)

Observation Day/Time/Lesson: _____

_____ **Videotaping.** (Recording a lesson and observing the lesson together with nonjudgmental questions prepared)

Observation Day/Time/Lesson: _____

Preparing to Observe: The Preconference

A supervision cycle usually consists of (1) a preconference, at which the process is discussed; (2) the observation, when the data are collected; and (3) a postconference for discussion and feedback about the lesson. At the first preconference you should be prepared to do the following:

_____ 1. Share the observation techniques and mutually agree on one you will use to observe the lesson. It's acceptable to be a novice at supervision and to share with the student teacher that you are a novice.

_____ 2. Discuss the specific purpose of the observation (i.e., to listen for questions, to look at movement, to videotape and look for facial expression, etc.). The more specific you are, the better. The two of you can decide which technique may be suited to the lesson and what particular aspect the student teacher might be interested in learning more about.

_____ 3. Have the student teacher share the lesson plan and any aspects of the lesson procedure with you at this time. This may include fears or anxieties about presenting the lesson.

_____ 4. Set up a time to have the postconference to review the data collected. List the date.

_____ 5. Decide what you will do with the data after they have been collected and reviewed.

Verbal Feedback

How does the student teacher use voice during the lesson? Select one or more approaches to use while observing a lesson. Graph paper is a good recording tool. List the date in front of the number to indicate you have observed.

_____ 1. **What Type of Question Is the Student Teacher Asking?** (Refer to ACT 6–7 for types.) List and categorize by types. You may also audiotape the lesson and after school have the student teacher list the categories instead of you doing it.

_____ 2. **Multiple Questions?** How often are questions being asked to the students, and how much wait time is there between questions? Often, higher-order questions need a longer time for students to process. Is the student teacher allowing that time? List the time the question is asked and how much wait time is allowed.

_____ 3. **Praise or Reprimand?** How does the student teacher verbalize behavior to encourage or discipline? List either positive/negative or both. Write the exact words and names of those students to whom verbal comments were made during the lesson.

_____ 4. **TTT—Teacher Talking Time?** Record how long the student teacher talks versus how long the students talk. Categorize the types of talking (e.g., lecturing, asking questions, giving directions [teacher]; answering questions, giving information, asking questions [students]).

_____ 5. **Gender Bias?** Record how many boys and how many girls participate during the lesson. Record the gender of those who raise their hands and then list who is called on and how often.

Movement during a Lesson

1. Observe the student teacher's movement during the lesson. Write brief descriptions of general movement patterns and times of most movement in the room.

    - Individual student movements

        Relating to one another

        Relating to the student teacher

    - Small groups of students

        Relating to one another

        Relating to the student teacher

    - Student teacher's movement around the room

2. Draw a diagram of the classroom and trace the student teacher's route during the lesson. Using various colors and a key, individual students' movements can also be traced on the same form. Graph paper may be used.

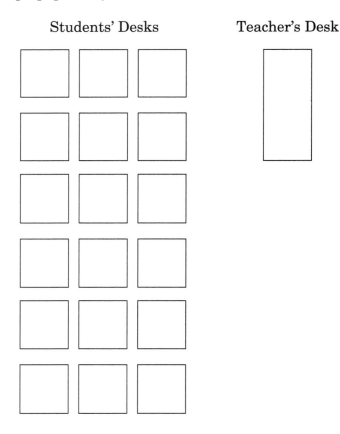

Students' Desks   Teacher's Desk

Focused Observation

As a cooperating teacher, it is important to give feedback to your student teacher regularly. Using the preconference and postconference will provide a formal time to share and discuss feedback. You can also use informal observation to observe and provide feedback. Your goal is to focus the student teacher on the teaching competencies and to use a common language to discuss teaching and learning. Refer to the college handbooks and the state certification language so that everyone is using the same terminology.

TIPS FOR INFORMAL OBSERVING

• Stay in the room as often as possible when your student teacher is teaching!

  You can learn a lot about his or her teaching style and how the students respond just by being in the room. Your students will notice you at first and come to you with questions, but if you strive to make yourself "invisible," you will be surprised at how quickly the students will direct their attention to the student teacher.

• Look for the ways your student teacher interacts with the students. Is he or she creating relationships? Is he or she treating them equally? Is he or she expecting high-quality work?

• Discuss with the student teacher and college supervisor when is the best time to leave the room. The student should not be left alone at the beginning of the semester.

• Write short notes while your student teacher is teaching and send them to him or her to encourage or guide him or her. This avoids your vocal interruptions.

Timing a Lesson

Use a stopwatch or a watch with a second hand to record how much time the student teacher spends on different parts of the lesson.

SAMPLE

Topic	Time Starts	Time Ends	Total
Introduction to lesson	_____	_____	_____
Giving directions	_____	_____	_____
Lecturing	_____	_____	_____
Answering questions	_____	_____	_____
Asking questions	_____	_____	_____
Practice work	_____	_____	_____
Reprimanding	_____	_____	_____
Checking for understanding	_____	_____	_____
Students actively engaged/ demonstrating learning	_____	_____	_____

What took up the most time during the lesson?

_____

_____

What took up the least time during the lesson?

_____

_____

Share this information with the student teacher and ask how the time spent relates to the original plan.

Audiotaping

During the practicum, the student teacher should audiotape several lessons and listen to them for a variety of reasons. As suggested in ACT 8–7, the student teacher could listen for types of questions, multiple questions, or wait time when asking questions. The student teacher may review audiotapes and check for the following:

_____ Level of vocabulary used during a lesson

_____ Tone of voice, clarity of voice

_____ How voice is used to reprimand

_____ How voice is used to praise

_____ Clarity of directions

_____ Repetition of information during the lesson

_____ Other:

_____ _____

You may want to assign one or more of these items to the student teacher for in-depth listening. In addition, a list of specific questions could be given to the student teacher to direct the listening. For example, you may suggest the student teacher listen to the tapes and answer the following questions:

1. How did the directions sound to you? Were they clear?

_____

2. How long did it take to give directions? Were they complicated? Two steps?

_____

_____

3. Do you think the students understood what to do? How do you know?

_____

_____

Videotaping

Encourage student teachers to be videotaped sometime during the practicum. More than once is preferred so the nervous reaction wears off and real teaching can be observed. As a cooperating teacher, you may want to be videotaped first, to model the process. It also shows you are willing to do the things you ask the student teacher to do. Another alternative may be to view teaching tapes sold by supervision companies, which provide a "neutral" teacher you can critique together.

Videotaping provides valuable information to the student teacher that audiotapes or data collection cannot show. It shows the real response to the lesson by the students in the class and the real presentation of the teacher. Often, student teachers (and classroom teachers) avoid taping because it shows all the blemishes of a teacher and a lesson. It is difficult to see at first, but once the initial personal reaction is over, the value of observing oneself cannot be denied. Also, videotapes are excellent additions to student teacher portfolios (see Chapter 16).

Before taping have a preconference with your student teacher and mutually agree on what should be taped and how the tape will be reviewed.

TWO WAYS TO USE VIDEOTAPES

_____ 1. Videotape the lesson for the student teacher and give it to him or her to review in privacy at home. Have a conference the next day and discuss the student teacher's reaction.

_____ 2. Videotape the lesson and set up a postconference with the student teacher to view the videotape together. Ask probing questions to have the student teacher share rather than pointing out what you noticed. Audiotape your postconference for future reference.

Cooperating Teacher's Reflection

How did you feel about supervising your student teacher?

JOURNAL ENTRY

Date: _____

_____

_____

_____

_____

_____

REFLECTIVE QUESTIONS

1. What did you learn about your own teaching as you collected data for your student teacher?

_____

_____

2. How did you feel about videotaping yourself/your student teacher?

_____

_____

3. What was the most difficult thing about supervising your student teacher?

_____

_____

Final Reminders and Helpful Hints

_____ Remember that the point of supervising is to observe your student teacher and assist him or her in growing, not to master the technique of observing.

_____ Don't worry if you are a beginner or have not mastered a technique or approach—be honest with the student teacher about your level of experience.

_____ Practice the techniques with a colleague to see how they work before trying them with the student teacher.

_____ Have the student teacher try some of the techniques on you! This lets him or her see what you will be doing when you observe.

_____ Be sure to preconference before doing any observation! It is important to be a partner with your student teacher. This collegiality will make you a more trusted mentor.

_____ Set up a postconference after observing. This should be as close as possible to the actual teaching of the lesson, or the next day at the latest. (See Chapter 9 for suggestions.)

_____ Write your own ideas on supervision techniques:

_____

_____

_____

_____

_____

_____

_____

_____

Conferencing and Giving Feedback

Remember that you are facilitating another person's process...facilitate what is happening rather than what you think ought to be happening.

John Heider

The purpose of this chapter is to give you some structure and support when evaluating your student teacher. The key to the quality of the practicum is the degree to which the cooperating teacher can share information so that personal feelings and personalities don't interfere. Any constructive criticism must be carefully expressed and balanced with positive comments to show where progress has been achieved.

Feedback can be given informally throughout the semester in the form of notes or verbal comments at the end of classes. Short notes can even be passed to a student teacher during a lesson if you see something really positive you want the student teacher to notice or something out of line that should be corrected immediately. This prevents a verbal interruption of the class, yet it allows you to communicate with the student teacher. Let the student teacher know you might do this from time to time and that it is a way of supporting rather than criticizing. Depending on the age of the students, you may also have to tell them you will be "passing notes" in class so they understand what you are doing. This can be an opportunity to praise (e.g., "Great job so far") and make a student teacher feel positive.

In addition, you may want to have your student teacher occasionally fill out a self-evaluation form. These forms can be attached to lesson plans along with any written feedback forms, handouts, or data collection forms and saved in a student teaching portfolio for future sharing or reflection.

Having regular times for informative conferences throughout the semester provides a consistent time for conversation and an opportunity for the student teacher to bring up specific aspects of the program that he or she needs to know more about. If there is any problem with the student teacher's teaching, it usually comes up at these conferences and can be dealt with. It is important to catch any difficulties early on in the experience. Daily short conferences can be scheduled if time permits. At this time, plans can be checked and positive affirmations given. A regularly scheduled time works best. Weekly conferences can be more involved and can include a review of college requirements or certification standards in addition to daily practice. Formal feedback given to your student teacher in a professional manner can avoid serious misunderstanding and can also assist the student teacher in growing to his or her full potential.

The forms, samples, and checklists in this chapter will assist you in designing successful conferences and giving feedback to your student teacher.

Lesson Plan

Time: After the student teacher has taught a lesson

Title: Conferencing with Your Student Teacher

Purpose: To provide immediate, honest feedback to the student teacher

Objectives:
- To understand the three types of conferences
- To avoid misunderstanding through communication
- To participate in a postconference or use a feedback form
- To set goals with the student teacher
- To reflect on and revise the process as needed

Procedure:
1. Design a plan for the three types of conferences.
2. Communicate with the student teacher and the supervisor.
3. Share observation data or other information.
4. Provide time for the student teacher to share and question.
5. Reflect on the experience.

Other Thoughts/ Notes: The conference is a critical component of the student teaching experience. Conferences do have different purposes. Be clear about the purpose of each conference before meeting with the student teacher to avoid misunderstandings.

University Supervisor Suggestions

PLAN: Organize your thoughts and materials, and prepare for your role.

Key Questions

1. How will you provide verbal and written feedback?

2. What do you need support and guidance in as you proceed?

Teaching Competency Focus Areas for Chapter 9

Knowledge, **Communication**, Instructional Practice, **Evaluation**, **Problem Solving**, Equity, & **Professionalism**

CONNECT: Use resources to enhance your skills as a supervisor.

People. Talk with an experienced supervisor to share techniques.

Books and Resources. Review ASCD videos, tapes, and books.

Technology. Create an on-line connection to the student teacher to provide instant feedback.

ACT: Select the activities that will be useful to you or create your own.

ACTion #1. Set up pre- and postconferences ahead of time.

ACTion #2. Use an agenda for your postconference. (See an example in this chapter.)

ACTion #3. Encourage the use of self-evaluation with the student teacher.

REFLECT: Think about your role as a supervisor and write a one-page reflection.

Choose to respond to the key questions on the previous page, create a prompt of your own, or answer the following question: How can I use the supervision feedback model to avoid misunderstandings?

Types of Conferences

Conferences can be organized into three categories. These categories are not necessarily definitive; they simply demonstrate that there are different purposes for different conferences.

1. Informative Conferences. These may take place at any time during the practicum and should be scheduled at a time that is convenient for both you and your student teacher. At the beginning of the practicum, they serve as orientation conferences at which information and expectations are discussed. The conference agenda should have room for addressing the student teacher's concerns. Dealing with curriculum issues, checking lesson plans, and discussing school issues are all part of this type of conference. Some cooperating teachers like to do this weekly at a regularly scheduled meeting; others like to do it informally as the needs arise.

When would you like to hold informative conferences with your student teacher? _____

_____

2. Feedback or Postobservation Conferences. These conferences are a follow-up to the supervision cycle in Chapter 8 or the discussion following the completion of the Feedback Form in this chapter. After supervising a specific lesson, you should meet with the student teacher to share the data or discuss the outcome of the lesson. There is an opportunity for real learning and reflection on the part of the student teacher if the conference is well planned with probing questions.

How many supervision cycles and postconferences would you like to do? _____

_____

How would you like to give written feedback to your student teacher? _____

_____

3. Three-Way Conferences. These are held with the college supervisor for the purpose of completing requirements. You should be an integral part of these conferences and should discuss the format with the supervisor beforehand. You may bring up issues and ideas at this time. If you have information that should be shared with the supervisor privately, set up an appointment for another time. This type of conference will also be discussed in the final chapter because it relates to completion of the student teaching experience.

List your questions for the 3-way conference:

_____

_____

_____

_____

List the topics you would like to discuss with the college supervisor:

_____

_____

_____

_____

How Do You Like to Receive Feedback?

Giving and accepting feedback is an important aspect of participating in a supervisory model. During student teaching, there will be times when you have to give critical feedback and praise to your student teacher. Before you share the information, whether it is positive or negative, think about how *you* like to receive feedback and be sensitive to how your student teacher may feel. Answer the following questions and use the answers as guidelines to think about how you will give feedback. This exercise may also provide an awareness for you as you think about providing either direct or objective feedback to the students in your classes.

1. Think of a time you received feedback as a child. Describe the situation. Who gave you the feedback?

_____

_____

Why do you think you recall this incident? What kind of feedback was it?

_____

_____

2. Think of a time recently that you received feedback. Describe the situation. Who gave you the feedback?

_____

_____

Why do you think you recall this incident? What kind of feedback was it?

_____

_____

How do you like to receive feedback? Do you like to give or receive feedback in writing so you can think about it? Do you like to give or receive verbal comments? Describe your "feedback style" here:

_____

_____

_____

Avoiding Misunderstandings

Before you give any feedback to your student teacher in any type of conference, you should think about the following questions. Jot your ideas down and share them with a colleague to gain more clarity for yourself. The important point here is to think about what is important to you and to communicate your ideas to the student teacher. The student teacher deserves to know what to expect regarding your methods of praising and giving feedback. If you are a person who holds off on praise until the end, that would be important to communicate to avoid frustrations and misunderstanding.

1. How will you praise your student teacher? If you don't praise consistently, will the student teacher think you didn't like a lesson? What is the role of praise in teaching? How do you like to have praise delivered? Should praise be specific? General? Verbal? Written?

   _____

   _____

   _____

2. How will you give criticism to your student teacher? How will it make a difference if the critical feedback relates to appropriate dress, interaction with students, verbal grammar, lesson planning, or some other issue? How do you like to receive critical feedback?

   _____

   _____

   _____

3. How will you use the nonjudgmental feedback cycle suggested in this handbook? Will you modify it? How? How will you integrate nonjudgmental observation with praise and critical feedback?

   _____

   _____

Asking Questions to Avoid Judgments

Instead of telling the student teacher what you think you saw, you should consider asking the student teacher to respond to some questions you ask. This promotes a more reflective dialogue and helps you avoid making judgments. There will be times when you will want to give direct feedback, but if it is mixed with questions, there will be less chance of judgmental comments. Making judgments on a student teacher's lessons is a delicate situation. Student teaching can be an anxiety-ridden experience. A voyage of self-discovery will bring the student teacher to new awareness levels about his or her teaching in a more positive manner without jeopardizing self-esteem.

QUESTIONS FOR A PRECONFERENCE

1. What is the purpose of the lesson?

2. How do you plan to engage the students?

3. Are you worried about any aspect of your plan?

4. Is there anything in particular you would like me to observe (e.g., how you give directions, whom you call on in the class, if you are using higher-order questions, etc.)?

5. How would you suggest I collect data?

6. _____

7. _____

QUESTIONS FOR A POSTCONFERENCE

1. How did your expectations for the lesson compare to the reality?

2. How did the students respond? Were they learning? How do you know?

3. What will you do differently or keep the same?

4. I noticed _____. Can you explain what you were thinking when that happened?

5. _____

6. _____

Sample Postconference Agenda

1. Introduce the conference/reactions.

    a. Discuss the upcoming conference (i.e., general response to being observed).

    b. Review the lesson plan.

2. Share the data.

    a. Review the technique you used.

    b. Share the information you collected with the student teacher.

3. Ask probing questions.

    a. Encourage student teacher inquiry (e.g., What do you think of this? How does this relate to what you thought was happening during the lesson? Why do you think this happened?).

    b. Initiate a discussion about teaching and the lesson.

4. Review the culmination of your lesson observation for one specific purpose.

    a. Review key learning points of student teacher inquiry.

    b. Set up another observation time to do the cycle again—ask what the student teacher would like you to observe and which technique to use.

5. Discuss the lesson in general.

    a. Review key points (e.g., clarity and knowledge of subject by student teacher).

    b. Share impressions (e.g., voice, movement, also content and sequence of the lesson).

    c. Share students' responses to lesson.

6. Ask the student teacher to self-reflect.

    a. What would you do differently next time you teach a lesson like this?

    b. What did you learn from this conference?

Using a Rubric for Assessing Progress

A student teaching rubric can be used to guide your discussions with the college supervisor and the student teacher. It is also a valuable way to have your student teacher self-assess during student teaching. Note competencies that are strong and those that need more attention. Review the rubric periodically to set goals with your student teacher. Work with the university supervisor to design the rubric that best represents the college preparation program and state competencies.

Example of Student Teaching Rubric for Instructional Practice

	Excellent Progress	Good Progress	Needs More Development	Needs Assistance	Unsatis-factory
Demonstrates creativity and thought in planning					
Uses a variety of teaching strategies and methods to engage learners					
Develops both long-form and short-form lesson plans					
Demonstrates principles and theories of instruction for students in the classroom					
Demonstrates proper sequencing and pacing of lessons					
Develops and modifies curriculum to meet student needs					
Manages the classroom alone in the role of teacher for short periods of time					
Handles difficult situations through problem-solving approaches					
Maintains an organized classroom for student learning					
Disciplines fairly					

Feedback Form

Date: _____

Subject/Grade: _____

Title of Lesson: _____

1. How well was the lesson plan written? Was it clear and easy to follow? Did it have a purpose that related to student learning?

_____

_____

2. How well did the student teacher carry out the lesson plan's objectives?

_____

_____

3. Describe one positive aspect of the lesson that demonstrates the student teacher's skills as a beginning teacher.

_____

_____

4. How were the students engaged during the lesson to encourage learning?

_____

_____

Commendations (positive aspects of teaching demonstrated):

_____

_____

Recommendations (suggestions for future lessons):

_____

_____

Other comments:

_____

_____

Goal Setting

_____ 1. During the conference, jointly select one aspect where the student teacher could strive for growth. This could be a "recommendation" from you or a goal offered by the student teacher.

_____ 2. Discuss specific actions the student teacher would have to take to grow in this area. List those actions.

_____ 3. Set a time when you will review this plan to see if the goal has been met. At that time, you may revise and continue with the same goal or select a new one and start the process again.

This form is for the student teacher.

GOAL	
ACTIONS What Will You Do to Achieve Your Goal?	
EVALUATION Date for Goal Review. How Will You Know if You Reach Your Goal?	

SAMPLE GOALS

Having interesting introductions to lessons

Culminating a lesson in an orderly way

Moving around the classroom

Pronouncing all the words in a lesson correctly

Managing an effective classroom routine during a lesson

Make the goal achievable, observable, and measurable!

Providing Helpful Feedback to Your Student Teacher

Student teachers want to know how they are doing. Most want to hear the praise and the "good news" daily, but many also want more regularly scheduled feedback, as well. Review your reflections on how you like to receive feedback and ask your student teacher how he or she would like to receive feedback from you. A weekly regularly scheduled time—even if it is only for 15 minutes—is an important component of supervising your student teacher. Try a variety of approaches throughout the semester.

Ways to Provide Feedback

	Verbal	*Written*	*Other*
Informal (once in a while)	• Talking after a lesson	• A short handwritten note ("Positive Postcard") for praise	• Audiotaping and letting student teacher listen and talk about his or her impressions
Informal (regular)	• Weekly meetings to talk about lessons and issues	• Keeping a journal and writing regular entries to the student teacher	
Formal (several times)	• Preconference and post conference discussions	• Data given to student teacher	• Videotaping of lesson and discussing together

Student Teacher Self-Evaluation

A student teacher may choose to self-evaluate on the lesson plans by making journal entries or by keeping a daily diary. This form is another way to have the student record his or her thoughts after a lesson is taught.

1. Did the students learn from my lesson? Were they actively engaged? How do I know?

_____

_____

2. How closely did I follow my lesson plan? Did I have to modify during the lesson? Why?

_____

_____

3. What do I think was the most effective part of the lesson?

_____

_____

4. Were the materials/visuals/aids appropriate? Why ? Why not?

_____

_____

5. What would I change/keep the same the next time I do this lesson?

_____

_____

6. What do I see as my teaching strengths?

_____

_____

7. A goal I would like to have my cooperating teacher assist me in reaching is:

_____

_____

Cooperating Teacher's Reflection

What stands out for you about giving your student teacher feedback?

JOURNAL ENTRY

Date: _____

_____

_____

_____

_____

_____

_____

_____

_____

REFLECTIVE QUESTIONS

1. What was the most difficult part about giving feedback and conferencing?

_____

_____

2. What skills/strengths do you possess as a cooperating teacher who gives feedback?

_____

_____

3. What did you learn about yourself in this process?

_____

_____

Final Reminders and Helpful Hints

_____ Remember to structure a feedback process with which both you and your student teacher are comfortable.

_____ Creating a trusting, open dialogue with your student teacher is a priority! Don't sacrifice the relationship for the structure. Create opportunities using the forms as guides for conversations.

_____ Pre- and postconferences are important opportunities to focus teaching conversations. This means that as a cooperating teacher, you have to stay in the room for certain periods and focus only on the student teacher's teaching.

_____ Self-evaluation for the student teacher is important. Encourage him or her to be consistent, but don't be unrealistic. You may also want to try to keep self-evaluations on your skills as a cooperating teacher giving feedback.

_____ Setting up regular times for feedback conferences in private locations will ensure they happen.

List some of your own ideas:

_____ _____

_____ _____

_____ _____

_____ _____

_____ _____

_____ _____

_____ _____

_____ _____

_____ _____

Information to Share with Your Student Teacher

Each of the chapters in this section includes forms, checklists, and questions that help the cooperating teacher *PLAN, ACT,* and *REFLECT* on the experience. Each chapter ends with a page that contains Final Reminders and Helpful Hints. This section builds on the relationship you have established with your student teacher and offers specific topics for discussion at some time during the practicum experience.

The four chapters in this section are: The Classroom as a Learning Environment, Classroom Management, Classroom Discipline, and Assessing, Recording, and Communicating Student Progress. This information may have been covered in the student teacher's college methods classes prior to the practicum experience. If that is the case, a brief review is all that may be necessary. If your student teacher appears to need more guidance in any of these topics, you can use the forms and checklists to guide your information-sharing sessions.

Use this section as a resource for discussion of these important aspects of teaching. Select the forms and checklists that you find most useful and feel free to create your own activities whenever necessary.

CHAPTER 10

The Classroom as a Learning Environment

*Life is either a daring adventure
or nothing at all.*

Helen Keller

An important part of being a good teacher is knowing the students in the classroom. Student teachers need to understand that the students are diverse in many ways. Nationality, religion, values, beliefs, personalities, physical abilities, academic abilities, habits, fears, and family support vary among the students. Other diversities also exist and need to be recognized for the value they add to the class as a whole. The students are important resources in the room, and they cannot share their unique qualities if the teacher is not aware of them.

It is important to bring students together so they can work as a team. Noting the multicultural aspects of the school and the community is critical in addressing the needs of the students in the classroom. The student teacher needs to understand the culture of the school and the broader community in which these students live. Being able to welcome diversity, such as recognizing different languages students speak, will be a positive asset in any student teacher's career.

The experience of diverse students broadens the sense of what really exists in the community surrounding the school and can enhance classroom discussions. The multiple perspectives provide a global sharing that can bring new awareness to all students in the classroom. This is especially important in urban classrooms with multiethnic perspectives. With schools becoming more diverse in their populations, teachers are challenged in new ways to include and value all students. Teachers and student teachers need to be sensitive to differences and be able to include them in the learning environment to create a community of learners.

One way students have been grouped has been by special needs and regular needs. These special needs sometimes include language support to learn English as a second language. Bilingual education and other programs to assist new students in speaking English may be part of your school's program. Share any of this information with your student teacher, even if your particular classroom is not involved this year. As student populations continue to become more diverse, especially in urban areas, beginning teachers need to become more aware of language support services.

Other support services have traditionally been available for students who are academically challenged. These students may have different learning styles or, for other reasons, are unable to keep the pace in a traditional classroom. In the past, these special students were pulled from regular classes and placed in smaller groups with special education teachers. Today, *inclusion* encourages schools to leave these students in the room. The rationale is that the social benefits and the models in the regular classroom assist these students in advancing more quickly. Some districts have classroom teachers coteach with a special education teacher. Inform your student teacher of the regulations around special education and any efforts that may exist around inclusion. Allow him or her to review education plans for individual students in your classes.

How your school groups students should also be discussed. Do you group by subject areas? Are you integrating subjects and crossing curriculum lines? Are there advanced placement classes? One way of valuing diverse multiethnic students has been to use interdisciplinary themes. Share your school's programs, policies, and goals and how they evolved to present practice.

Valuing diverse student populations, including special education and regular education students in one classroom, and grouping students by abilities are ways in which learning environments are created. Discuss your personal philosophy around each of these issues. You may also want to include a conversation about how equity and social justice relate to building communities of learners.

A discussion of learning styles and teaching styles would also be appropriate at this time. Recognizing students' learning styles will encourage the student teacher to change his or her teaching style to create a learning environment.

Encourage your student teacher to talk with other teachers or administrators in the building to hear other points of view. This will support the understanding that there may not always be agreement in a school around some of these issues. These are complex issues with emotional points of view. Support your student teacher in gathering information from many sources so he or she can be an informed participant in future discussions related to these issues.

Lesson Plan

Time: As the student teacher begins teaching the whole class

Title: Creating a Learning Environment with Diverse Learners

Purpose: To recognize the diverse populations in a classroom and school and to take into account these differences when planning lessons and creating a learning environment for all students.

Objectives:
- To develop an awareness of multicultural gifts
- To recognize grouping strategies
- To develop knowledge of special education policies and procedures
- To learn strategies for developing a community of learners
- To make suggestions for modifying academic instruction
- To develop sensitivity to teaching locations (urban, suburban, rural)

Procedure:
1. Brainstorm with your student teacher about diversity.
2. Create a class profile.
3. Discuss learning environments with all types of diversity.
4. Suggest possible strategies for modifying lessons.

**Other Thoughts/
Notes:** The student teacher needs to know and respect who is in the class-

room. School is not simply for imparting information anymore.

Rather, it is a learning environment made up of many types of

learners.

University Supervisor Suggestions

PLAN: **Organize your thoughts and materials, and prepare for your role.**

Key Questions

1. How does your student teacher build a community of learners?

2. How do teaching and learning styles relate to this community?

Teaching Competency Focus Areas for Chapter 10

Knowledge, Communication, Instructional Practice, Evaluation, Problem Solving, **Equity,** & Professionalism

---

CONNECT: **Use resources to enhance your skills as a supervisor.**

People. Ask the student teacher to interview the cooperating teacher or the principal.

Books and Resources. Diversity, equity, and mulitculturalism should be reviewed.

Technology. Try multicultural book reviews: www.isomedia.com

ACT: **Select the activities that will be useful to you or create your own.**

ACTion #1. Assist the student teacher in creating a sociogram to learn about his or her class.

ACTion #2. Share your teaching style with the student teacher.

ACTion #3. Discuss possible team and community building activities.

REFLECT: **Think about your role as a supervisor and write a one-page reflection.**

Choose to respond to the key questions on the previous page, create a prompt of your own, or answer the following question: How can I support my student teacher in creating learning communities and why is this important?

Creating a Classroom Profile

Ask your student teacher to create a profile of the students in your classroom. If you are teaching secondary or middle school, select one of your classes. He or she can find the information about the students by observing, reviewing their class records, taking a written survey, conducting interviews, creating a class questionnaire, or talking with you. The more a teacher knows about the class, the easier it is to create and maintain a positive learning environment.

Student	Gender	Culture	Age	Language	Musical Ability	Artistic Ability	Athletic Ability	Learning Style	Learning Need	?

After completing the chart, review the data with your student teacher and think about the ways these students can contribute to the creation of a positive learning environment.

Constructing and Using a Sociogram

One way to illustrate the dynamics in a classroom is to construct a sociogram. Do this with your student teacher to gain insights into the work preferences of the students. You can use the information to design cooperating groups or teams. It will also let you know what the students think of each other and where you may have to step in to include some students that you may not have realized were excluded.

Step 1 Ask students in the classroom to list three students—by first, second, and third choice—that they would prefer to work with in the classroom. (Make a distinction between work partners and social partners outside of school.) Tell them it is for possible future group projects and that you may use it to create teams with at least one person with whom they prefer to work.

Step 2 Have the students write the reason they selected each of their choices. This will give you some insight, and themes may repeat themselves.

Step 3 Collect the data and make a grid with students' names across the top and down the left side. Graph paper works well. Place a 1, 2, or 3 under the student's name as indicated to show choices.

EXAMPLE

	Adam	Michael	Sue	Laura
Adam	—	1st	3rd	2nd
Michael	3rd	—	1st	2nd
Sue	3rd	2nd	—	1st
Laura	3rd	2nd	1st	—

Step 4 Tally choices to indicate most preferred working partners (commonly called *stars*) and least selected working partners (referred to as *isolates*).

Step 5 Use a square for boys and a triangle for girls and cut the shapes to represent each student in your class. Place on a poster board to illustrate how students made choices. Draw arrows with choice number pointed to student. Using three colors for 1, 2, and 3 works well. The visual display will illustrate stars and isolates.

NOTE: THIS IS A CONFIDENTIAL PROCESS—NOT TO BE SHARED WITH STUDENTS.

SAMPLE OF FIRST CHOICES

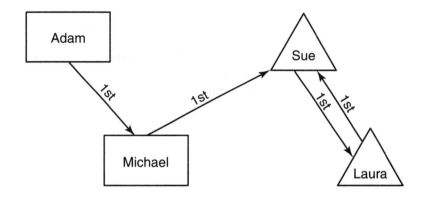

This is a good exercise for the cooperating teacher and student teacher to do together.

1. Read the choices and reasons why students selected preferred working partners. Were there any surprises? Were there common themes for selecting students? What else did you notice?

_____

_____

_____

_____

_____

2. Review the data on the grid and write your initial impressions of how it describes the classroom relationships. Discuss and compare to the cooperating teacher's impressions.

_____

_____

_____

_____

_____

_____

3. Build the sociogram using triangles and squares. After the symbols have been placed on poster board, glue and draw arrows indicating preferences.

Teaching Styles: Which Do You Prefer?

An awareness level of your teaching style and how it matches your students' learning styles is important. Your student teacher needs to understand how teaching styles and learning styles relate. Answer the following questions with your student teacher and compare your responses. Notice that certain styles of teaching bring out certain learners in the classroom. How you "prefer" to teach is usually based on what you find most comfortable.

- Do you like to talk and explain concepts to students verbally?

    Then you probably...

    ...lecture for a major part of the class period

    ...talk to students

    Students who prefer auditory learning will respond.

- Do you like to write and see concepts on paper?

    Then you probably...

    ...use the board to list ideas

    ...write outlines for students

    ...create study guides

    ...ask students to take notes

    Students who prefer to see things in writing will respond.

- Do you enjoy using visual displays?

    Then you probably...

    ...use the computer to demonstrate a concept

    ...bring in models and posters to show students

    ...use webbing and graphic organizers

    Students who prefer pictures and drawings will respond.

- Do you like to touch and see things happen?

    Then you probably...

    ...create experiments for your classroom

    ...design hands-on lesson with manipulatives

...bring things to show and tell about

Students who want to "touch" and observe the activity will respond.

As teachers, we need to demonstrate all these styles in our classroom even though we are comfortable with certain styles, as evidenced by the previous questions. Students in our classrooms will have a variety of learning styles and preferred styles. Once you discover the students' styles and multiple intelligence, you will need to be sure that your student teacher adapts and varies his or her teaching so that all students will respond. Remember, the goal is to have students learn to respond to as many styles of teaching as possible.

How would you describe your preferred style? What is your student teacher's preferred style?

_____

_____

How can two styles in one classroom actually benefit the students in the room?

_____

_____

How can all the styles be utilized to maximize student learning in your classroom?

_____

_____

Documenting Learning Styles

Learning styles: Recognizing differences. Students learn in many ways. Being able to recognize the differences will assist the student teacher in designing lessons and bringing the students together as a team. Diversity of learning styles makes the team more resourceful, yet members of the class need to also be aware of the differences so they don't argue about their different approaches.

Check your own preferred learning styles and compare with your student teacher. Share current learning-style theories with the student teacher and assist in translating that theory into practice by observing students. Many of these theorists have short learning-style tests that are available for use. Check with the school guidance counselor or adjustment counselor for details.

Have the student teacher ask the students how they think they learn best. Students know what they prefer and which methods work best for them. Encourage the student teacher to think of ways to train students to build on their own learning strengths so they can adjust conditions to suit them. This is very helpful when a teacher has large class sizes. This doesn't mean they should never use other approaches—in fact, as a teacher or student teacher, you should be assisting students in becoming more comfortable with several learning styles.

1. Review your students to see which are primarily:

    ___auditory   ___visual   ___hands-on   ___random

    ___sequential   ___inductive   ___deductive

    Most students are a combination of several but have a preferred approach.

2. Interview several students in the classroom about their preferred learning style. Ask the students why they prefer this style. If they use a combination, list them.

Student   **Preferred Style(s) and Reason**

_____   _____

_____   _____

_____   _____

3. Note current learning-style theory here and list any key points that will assist you in teaching.

_____

4. Notes and observations about learning styles:

_____

_____

_____

_____

_____

_____

_____

_____

_____

_____

Using Varied Teaching Styles

_____   • **Use both auditory and visual directions.** Students in the classroom may be auditory or visual learners. Giving directions in both written and oral form will include these varied learners. Also, be aware of giving multiple directions, especially orally, that students of varied levels may not be able to retain. Write directions on the board or overhead projector and leave them up throughout an activity so they can be referred to at any time.

_____   • **Demonstrate concepts by using visual examples.** After directions are given and the student teacher feels students understand, specific examples should be given to concretely show what is expected. This does not mean students are supposed to copy the example. It is to provide a visual prop that is used by the student teacher or classroom teacher to demonstrate what is expected.

_____   • **Allow for choice when appropriate.** If possible, provide several activities that meet the same objective and allow students to choose the one with which they feel most comfortable. *Example:* If the goal is to solve a word problem in math, choices for solving could include paper and pencil, manipulatives, working alone, or working with a partner. The point is that you want the students to use their best learning style to solve the problem.

_____   • **Plan for varied paces.** Students think and work at different speeds. The faster thinkers are not necessarily the most accurate or the most creative problem solvers. Don't be trapped by rewarding only the quickest students, because you may be missing some outstanding problem solving. Sometimes it is appropriate to leave a task incomplete. Doing a portion of some math problems can show you whether the students understand the concept.

_____   • **Assist students who need support.** Some students will need additional support during a lesson because they do not understand the directions or are unable to complete the task. You may not have time to walk around the room and meet with these students individually. One strategy is to let them work with a partner who is able to explain more clearly what is expected. These "partner coaches" can be selected before class begins, and they do not have to have their own work done to assist.

Sometimes students who finish early are used as "coaches" for students who may need extra support. Be careful though—this could look as if you want all students to finish early. Another approach is to bring students having difficulty to you in a small-group situation. Not only can you save time by saying things once; the group members can then support each other once they understand the concept.

_____ • **Provide optional enrichment for students who finish early and understand the concepts.** Students who complete the assignment and fully understand the lesson may finish early and be a distraction to others who need more time. One way to involve them for the rest of the class time is to offer several "challenge" problems or activities that take more effort. These can be placed on the board or on a handout. Another way is to set up predetermined learning stations in the classroom and allow students to select one to work at for the rest of the period. For middle school or high school, you may prefer to encourage the students to manage their own time and use it to read or complete homework. Enrichment time should be optional as long as the students are engaged in some activity of their choice. More of the same original activity is not recommended because students will quickly notice that a faster pace just gets more of the same.

_____ • **Write your own idea here.**

Team Building: Creating a Community of Learners

Discuss the following approaches to team building and check those the student teacher wants to try.

_____ **1. Sharing time.** Students come to school with a lot on their minds. If it is appropriate, allow for a short period of time every day to let students listen to one another. Use this as an opportunity to have students be good listeners and speakers. Plus, the conversation is real life!

_____ **2. Partners.** At all grade levels, students are absent or miss parts of a school day. Assigning partners encourages students to care about each other and take responsibility for the academic material. In secondary school, a log may be more appropriate than partners. This lists homework assignments and other information important to the class. Absent students read it the day they come in and can talk to the log writer.

_____ **3. Teams.** Within the classroom create small learning teams for various activities or projects. Let the teams create names, slogans, and strategies for completing assignments. Rotate teams often so the individuals in the class as a whole have many opportunities to work with different students. You may want to create the teams yourself at first to make sure all students are included and that team making doesn't become a popularity contest. One strategy for knowing your classroom and making teams is using the sociogram technique (see PLAN 10-4).

_____ **4. Compliments.** At the end of the day or a class period, have students recognize one another through compliments. You or the student teacher may need to model appropriate compliments before students know how to do it. A student who receives a compliment must acknowledge it by saying thank you.

Cooperating Teacher's Reflection

How does your teaching style affect your students' learning?

JOURNAL ENTRY

Date: _____

_____

_____

_____

_____

_____

_____

_____

REFLECTIVE QUESTIONS

1. What have I learned about my own teaching in the process of sharing about learning environments with my student teacher?

   _____

   _____

2. What are my strengths in teaching and modifying to meet the needs of all learners?

   _____

   _____

3. How does my learning style compare to my teaching style?

   _____

   _____

Final Reminders and Helpful Hints

_____ Work with the student teacher on this chapter. You have the information to create the class profile and categories that include all your students. Don't expect the student teacher to do this alone.

_____ This is not a chapter to be memorized, but more of a process of awareness that should let the student teacher realize who the audience is for the lessons he or she is designing.

_____ Be clear about your own biases regarding differences and notice how you share this information with your student teacher. If you think you have a biased opinion on any issue, be sure to let the student teacher talk with another teacher with a different point of view.

_____ Assist the student teacher in incorporating academic modification into daily planning. The strategies for modifying may become more overwhelming than the lesson itself. The awareness of differences is as important as the teacher techniques for modifying lessons. Coach the student teacher to keep the awareness, and the techniques will come.

_____ All differences do not require modification; however, student differences do need to be recognized and all students included. They can bring rich resources to class discussions (e.g., foreign exchange students, bilingual students, musical talents, etc.).

_____ Discuss why it is important to recognize differences in the classroom and how this awareness can enhance a teacher's effectiveness.

_____ List your final reminders below:

_____

_____

_____

_____

CHAPTER 11

Classroom Management

*Classroom management sets the stage
for a positive learning climate. You reap
what you sow.*

Gail Dion

Setting up a classroom and establishing a routine are essential to good teaching. Student teachers who begin the practicum experience in the fall semester have the benefit of seeing how an experienced teacher sets up a classroom and establishes a routine. Student teachers who practice teach in the spring do not observe this process. This chapter is designed to have you share valuable information about your management style and routines in an organized way, whether it is in the fall or the spring practicum.

You must remember it has taken years to refine your routine and management techniques. Your student teacher is being asked to jump into your established routine or to watch you set it up. The student teacher is with you only for a short period of time, and it is sometimes difficult for two people to work under a management system that has been totally designed by only one of the people on the team. Be sensitive to this and if possible ask the student teacher what he or she thinks about any of your procedures. Sometimes an outside view can solve a problem you have been grappling with for some time.

Classroom management involves (1) setting up the physical space of the classroom, (2) establishing a routine, (3) setting boundaries/rules, and (4) maintaining a level of attention from students. Each of these contributes to the overall management system in your classroom and requires some explanation for your student teacher. All these areas require careful thought and planning, but they often appear to just "happen" in the classroom.

Classroom management is usually associated with discipline. Explain to your student teacher that setting a positive climate, establishing routines, and using creative ideas to prevent discipline problems is different from disciplining students who have broken rules or been disruptive. An effective management system can deter many potential discipline problems, but there will probably still be a few. (Chapter 12 is devoted to discipline issues.)

Probably the most discussed aspect of a routine is being able to gain the attention of the students in the classroom. It is often called *classroom control* and implies that the teacher actually controls the students to make them listen. This is not the case, and student teachers who try to do this are often frustrated and misled into believing they can control a class. Even though we, as cooperating teachers, often use the term, our real objective is to have the students want to listen and be motivated to hear about the lesson and activities. This sometimes takes an enthusiastic presentation style and use of many techniques. Maintaining the students' interest throughout the class lesson is as important as gaining the attention at the beginning of a lesson. The best-designed lessons are not useful learning experiences if the students are not behaving appropriately.

In addition to the aspects of management listed here, it is important to note that teacher attitude is an overriding factor in designing an organized classroom. Respect for differences, fair treatment of students, and a pleasant presentation style all make a difference. Discuss these issues with your student teacher and point out ways you model positive attitude to maintain and gain the attention of your students.

The forms and checklists in this chapter can be modified for elementary and secondary classrooms. Use your judgment to select the ideas that are most appropriate for your grade level.

Lesson Plan

Time: Beginning to middle of the practicum

       Title: Classroom Management

    Purpose: To share techniques that work and to make the student teacher aware of the importance of management to create an organized learning environment with few disruptions

  Objectives:
- To create awareness of behind-the-scenes organization
- To have optimal teaching/learning take place
- To share ideas and use the student teacher as a resource

  Materials: Forms in this chapter

  Procedure:
1. Document successful ideas and share them with the student teacher.
2. Use the action forms in this chapter for specific aspects.
3. Review and reflect on all techniques being used.

Other Thoughts/ Notes: Discuss with your student teacher any management techniques you have used in the past that you have discontinued and explain why. Discuss why some things work some years and not other years and how you have adapted techniques to make them more successful.

University Supervisor Suggestions

> **PLAN:** Organize your thoughts and materials, and prepare for your role.

Key Questions

1. How will you inventory what the student teacher already knows?

2. How will you highlight key areas of management?

Teaching Competency Focus Areas for Chapter 11

Knowledge, Communication, Instructional Practice, Evaluation, **Problem Solving, Equity,** & Professionalism

> **CONNECT:** Use resources to enhance your skills as a supervisor.

People. Ask the student teacher to talk with other teachers at his or her grade level for ideas.

Books and Resources. Review classroom management books for more ideas to suggest.

Technology. Check the New Teacher Page at www.geocities.com

> **ACT:** Select the activities that will be useful to you or create your own.

ACTion #1. Bring a group of student teachers together to share success stories.

ACTion #2. Share the ideas you have seen work in the past with other student teachers.

ACTion #3. Organize a sharing session with a group of cooperating teachers so they can share, too!

> **REFLECT:** **Think about your role as a supervisor and write a one-page reflection.**

Choose to respond to the key questions on the previous page, create a prompt of your own, or answer the following question: How effective am I in assisting my student teacher in viewing many types of classroom management strategies?

Using Classroom Space

Ask your student teacher to complete the following chart for the level at which you are teaching. If there are several teachers at the same grade level in your school, the student teacher can observe informally to see if he or she follows the same guiding principles for organizing the physical environment of his or her classroom. Ask the student teacher to note why it might be different. You might want to extend this activity to see how space arrangements vary from grade level by interviewing other teachers and filling in the rest of this chart. Note that one teacher's response cannot be generalized to say that *all* middle school teachers would do it this way.

	Early Childhood	*Elementary*	*Middle School*	*High School*
Student Desks How are they organized? Why?				
Teacher's Desk Where is it placed? Why?				
Bulletin Boards or Learning Centers How are they used? Why?				
Supplies and Materials Where are they located? Who gets to touch them? Why?				
Computer(s) Where are they? How are they used? Why?				
Other?				

Establishing Routines and Why They Are Important

Routines are important for maintaining consistency and moving through a teaching day in a manner that students can expect. Discuss the following with your student teacher as you share your classroom routines:

1. What are the purposes of the routines?

2. Are the students familiar with the routines?

3. How do you reinforce a routine already established?

4. How do you introduce a new routine to the class?

5. What other skill(s) are students learning while participating in daily routines

6. Are routines saving time that can be used for teaching?

ROUTINE CATEGORIES AND EXAMPLES

1. Examples of *opening routines* at beginning of day or class:

   - Attendance and how to handle students who are absent so they get work

   - Lunch count

   - Collecting homework and recording it

2. Examples of *operating procedures:*

   - Walking to classes

   - Leaving during class time

   - Fire drills

3. Examples of *teaching routines:*

   - Expected behavior in classroom

   - Class discussion procedures for listening to others

   - Noise level for group work

   - Students who forgot books or materials

   - What activities students who finish early may do

4. Examples of *closing routines* at beginning of day or class:

   • Collecting work

   • Leaving classroom

   • Cleaning up

5. List other routines used in this classroom.

_____

_____

_____

Rules, Rewards, and Consequences

Rules, rewards, and consequences are part of a teacher's management system. Since they vary significantly by grade and age of students, it is important for the student teacher to understand and observe them. Share with your student teacher how your rules, rewards, and consequences were established. Did students have any input in creating them? How long have you been using this system? What other systems have you used in the past? Why did you change? The key to rules, rewards, and consequences is communicating them to the students *before* the rules are broken. Ask the student teacher to complete this chart for the appropriate grade level. How effectively would your rules, rewards, and consequences transfer to other grade levels?

	Early Childhood	*Elementary*	*Middle School*	*High School*
Rules: What are they? Who created them? Are they visibly displayed?				
Rewards: What are they? Material items? Verbal praise? No homework? When are rewards given? Do they work? Do they match the rules?				
Consequences: What are they? How often are they used? Do they fit the misbehavior? Are they grade-level appropriate?				

Gaining and Maintaining Student Attention

Teachers need to have students' attention at various times during the day to give instructions, to move the class to another room, to make announcements, and so on. Ask your student teacher to observe how you gain and maintain attention for these noninstructional activities.

STARTING THE CLASS PERIOD OR SCHOOL DAY/ BEGINNING THE LESSON

Integrating noninstructional announcements, collection of homework, opening exercises, and so on, often take place at the beginning of the school day or class period. How do you do this? How is it included in the time allotted for the lesson?

How do you initially gain students' attention to shift from noninstructional announcements to instructional curriculum? Do you use a story? A prop? A question? Do you connect what is coming up in the lesson to the students' own experiences?

THE LESSON

How do you maintain this attention while teaching the whole class? If there are small groups, is it different? How do you ensure all students are engaged in a learning experience? Do you walk around? How do you interact with students to keep them on task? Do you call on students? List any maintaining management strategies you use here and share with your student teacher.

_____

_____

ENDING THE CLASS PERIOD/CLOSING THE LESSON

How do you complete the lesson? How do you know the students learned? How do you check for understanding? Are there noninstructional directions that need to be given at the end of class? Is there time for questions and answers, or does the lesson just end? Is there time for students to do homework? How do you close the lesson and end the class period? How do these things differ (e.g., closing the lesson as opposed to ending the class at the bell)? List the management closing techniques for closing you will share here.

_____

_____

How does opening, maintaining, and closing a lesson in a predictable and organized way contribute to student learning?

_____

_____

_____

Discuss these issues with your student teacher and write your thoughts here.

_____

_____

_____

_____

_____

_____

_____

Cooperating Teacher's Reflection

What have you learned about yourself in the process of sharing your management system?

JOURNAL ENTRY

Date: _____

_____

_____

_____

_____

_____

REFLECTIVE QUESTIONS

1. How does your classroom management system enhance your teaching?

_____

_____

2. What have you noticed about your student teacher's management skills?

_____

_____

3. What would you highlight as the most important management skill a teacher needs to have and use?

_____

_____

Final Reminders and Helpful Hints

_____ Remember the student teacher will not be able to do all of these things immediately—your skills have been refined over time.

_____ Setting up a classroom is a matter of individual style. The student teacher may not agree with your philosophy or reasoning for a classroom set-up. Be open to his or her views. Allow the student teacher to try some ideas if they are not disruptive to your established routine.

_____ Rules are boundaries for students within the school and the classroom. Be sure you consistently model the same rules. For example, teachers should not chew gum if the students' rule is no gum chewing.

_____ Let your student teacher observe and question why you do things a certain way. Make some time to answer these questions.

_____ Allow your student teacher to visit other rooms and document how those teachers set up the classroom and manage routines. Ask the student teacher to share this information with you!

_____ List your helpful hints below:

_____

_____

_____

_____

_____

CHAPTER 12

Classroom Discipline

Anticipate problems before they happen.
Nancy Legan

In theory, if a teacher organizes an effective classroom, designs lessons that meet the needs of all students, and presents information creatively, there should be no need for disciplining students. However, there are cases where students break rules and must face consequences. Most of the time, the consequences are clear and there is not a repeat break of the rule. Sometimes a student misbehaves and there is not a particular rule or consequence established. This is when a teacher must make a decision about how to handle the situation. As a teacher, you must remind the student teacher to be fair and consistent.

Discipline often relates to three areas: students being on task, students demonstrating responsible behavior, and students respecting others. When these things are not happening in a positive way, there may be discipline problems. The problems may require different responses from the teacher. Someone sleeping in the back of the room is certainly not on task, but it is very different from two students having a fistfight. They both require a conversation and some action on the part of the teacher; however, the fight needs an immediate response, whereas the teacher may decide to have a conversation with the sleeping student at the end of class. Discuss situations with your student teacher that need immediate responses, as opposed to those that can wait.

Remind the student teacher that students who are actively engaged in the learning process are less likely to become behavior problems. (A review of Chapters 5 and 11 may be appropriate here.)

Teachers often use two basic approaches to disciplining students in the classroom. One is more student centered and the other teacher centered. The student approach involves the students in the design of the rules; in some classrooms, the students even assist the teacher in implementing consequences. This type of classroom places the responsibility on the students. The teacher and the students work more as partners than as in a hierarchical relationship.

The teacher-centered classroom is more authoritarian and traditional. With this approach, the teacher is the authority who makes and implements all the rules. The students just respond. The student teacher should be aware of both approaches, and you should be prepared to explain your approach. If you find you use a combination of the two, make sure the student teacher understands this and how you explain your discipline policies to your students. Also, share how the school rules and policies relate to your classroom system and when and how you decide to involve the principal.

In addition to these basic approaches, you should point out that there are at least two strategies for responding to misbehavior. One is to respond to some positive behavior taking place in the room, and another is to respond to the behavior itself. For example, if a student is tipping in a chair, the positive strategy would be to ignore the specific behavior and say, " I see most of you are sitting up the way I have asked you to. Thank you for doing that." In most cases, that student would get the message and put the chair down.

The strategy that responds to the behavior would have the teacher either verbally say something directly to the student or move closer to give a signal that showed it was not desired behavior. Neither is right or wrong. It may be more effective to use one strategy over another at different times. It should be realized that disciplining by pointing out misbehavior all day can be a tiring and overwhelming experience for a student teacher, so mixing the strategies is worth considering.

Your student teacher also needs to distinguish between daily classroom rules and consequences, repeated misbehaviors, attention getting (a student who may be fooling around with other classmates) and other disruptions of a more serious nature. Consequences should be positive, not punitive, to help the students learn the proper behavior. Designing progressive consequences for repeat behavior may be appropriate—for example, the first-time consequence is . . . ; the second time, it is . . . ; after that, expect. . . . A student who forgets homework once may be different from a student who repeatedly forgets to do homework. The goal is to teach the students to bring their homework, not to punish them for not doing it.

The student teacher needs to know when a more serious disciplinary action is necessary, and you should be involved in helping make the distinction. A very different response may be required when a student is clowning in class and making jokes than when a student damages another student's property. Both are certainly distracting behaviors, but each requires a different disciplinary action on the part of the teacher. If a note to parents is required, you will need to decide if you and your student teacher will cosign it. Decide at the beginning of the practicum whether you will cosign all parent communication with your student teacher, so you won't have any surprises.

You may need to assist the student teacher in applying an appropriate punishment for a misbehavior. In an effort to be fair, some student teachers use the same punishment for any disruption during a class. For example, staying after school would be the consequence for students who are fighting, or who forget their homework, or who shout out in class. Sometimes the students in the classroom don't see the same consequence as fair and may note the punishment does not fit the crime. Discuss fair and equitable consequences and use examples and anecdotes that will help your student teacher see the distinctions between major issues and minor problems.

Teachers today have to be concerned about violence in schools. The student teacher must be aware of and understand all school policies and rules regarding student threats, weapons in school, and so on. Detention rooms and the concepts of school-based discipline programs should be shared with the student teacher even if you are not directly involved. Safety issues should be discussed honestly, and the student teacher should be made aware of any potentially dangerous students or situations. Student teachers need to know if their personal items need to be locked when not in use or if the parking lot is prone to vandalism.

Your school principal may be the person who handles the more serious problems. A meeting between your student teacher and the principal may be helpful in explaining how to recognize when a student needs to be sent out of the room. When to report a student to the office and the criteria for expulsion should be included in your discussion if appropriate.

It is difficult to teach someone how to discipline a student in every instance, because often each situation may be unique. Share your most effective strategies and the guidelines you use to make difficult disciplinary decisions. Your goal during the practicum should be to maintain consistent discipline procedures so the students are not responding one way to you and another way to the student teacher. Discuss how your discipline strategies have evolved and developed over the years. It may be helpful to let the student teacher know if you ever had difficulty with discipline and how you handled these situations.

Disciplining students for misbehavior plays another role in teaching, because all of the students watch a teacher do it. How you respond to misbehavior will set the tone in a classroom. Students often label teachers for their disciplinary style ("She's a screamer," "He always kicks you out of class," "She lets you get away with everything," etc.). Make sure the student teacher realizes "everyone" watches when there is an interaction between a student and a teacher in a classroom. The other students are making judgments that could lead to future discipline problems. The student teacher has to learn this valuable skill "on the job" with you there assisting.

Most student teachers don't often get to observe a teacher handling discipline problems. One reason for this is that experienced teachers usually know how to ward off many of these problems and misbehaviors before they even happen. You will not have the same behavior problems in a classroom with the same students that the student teacher has. Your experience and subtle body language cues give you fewer observable discipline problems. This can be frustrating to the student teacher because when he or she takes over the class, the students take advantage. Be prepared to share the subtle cues you use that stop a misbehavior before it happens.

Student teachers often come to the practicum experience wanting to be liked by their students, and consequently they start out being a friend rather than a teacher. Discuss the issue of friendship with your student teacher. Warn him or her that some students may "test" the friendship and that he or she should be prepared with ways to deal with relationship issues.

Short daily conferences that highlight ways you handled specific problems with students are always helpful. If a daily conference is not possible, jot down any situations and share when you can. You may want to share all the information in this chapter with your student teacher early on in the experience.

The forms, samples, and checklists in this chapter will assist you in sharing and discussing this important topic.

Lesson Plan

Time: As part of daily conferences

Purpose: To have the student teacher observe, discuss, and implement fair discipline techniques

Objectives:
- To prevent discipline problems
- To provide questions to think about
- To provide tips for disciplining
- To create awareness of legal aspects

Materials: Forms in this handbook

Procedure:
1. Discuss your philosophy and style of discipline.
2. Review cases, tips, and questions to think about.
3. Discuss the legal aspects of discipline.
4. Reflect on your discussion.

Other Thoughts/ Notes: Let the student teacher observe and talk with as many teachers and administrators as possible regarding discipline. Even though there are guidelines, people have different interpretations. Have the student teacher keep a notebook of successful techniques or strategies. Many of these strategies are preventive techniques that relate to classroom management and routine.

University Supervisor Suggestions

PLAN: **Organize your thoughts and materials, and prepare for your role.**

Key Questions

1. What are the discipline philosophies of the school and your student teacher?

2. What is your discipline philosophy and how does it relate to the question above?

Teaching Competency Focus Areas for Chapter 12

Knowledge, Communication, Instructional Practice, Evaluation, **Problem Solving, Equity,** & Professionalism

CONNECT: **Use resources to enhance your skills as a supervisor.**

People. Who can assist the student teacher in learning more about discipline?

Books and Resources. Suggest a few specific books (from the many on the market) to your student teacher.

Technology. Go to the website 10 Ways to Help Kids Pay Attention: www.nea.org/neatoday

ACT: **Select the activities that will be useful to you or create your own.**

ACTion #1. Role-play with the student teacher how to handle difficult situations.

ACTion #2. Create case studies or use the ones in this text to think about difficult issues.

ACTion #3. Create a "problems to possibilities" seminar and invite a group of student teachers.

REFLECT: **Think about your role as a supervisor and write a one-page reflection.**

Choose to respond to the key questions on the previous page, create a prompt of your own, or answer the following question: How can I assist my student teacher in understanding the importance of handling discipline issues fairly?

What Is Your Discipline Philosophy?

1. What is the philosophy you operate under in your own classroom? Define *discipline* for your student teacher. How do you know when you must discipline a student?

_____

_____

_____

2. How does your philosophy relate to and blend with the school's rules for disciplining?

_____

_____

_____

3. List specific reasons for sending a student to the principal's office.

_____

_____

_____

4. Give an example of a situation that could be handled two different ways and tell why. Use a real situation you have been involved with if possible.

_____

_____

_____

Questions to Think about Before Disciplining a Student

Discuss the following with the student teacher to use as a guide.

1. Who is the student?

   - Does this student have a prearranged plan when he or she is disruptive (e.g., sent to guidance, principal, or resource or learning center classroom)?

   - Is this a first offense or is this repeated misbehavior?

   - Does this student have a special need that has not been addressed?

   - Are there other adults that need to be notified when this student is disruptive?

2. What rule did the student break?

   - Is it a major offense (hitting someone, possession of weapon)?

   - Is it a minor offense (gum chewing, wearing a hat)?

   - Is it related to academic work (not doing homework, cheating)?

   - Is it related to work habits (not listening in class)?

3. What did the student specifically do or say?

4. Is this misbehavior appropriate for the student's age?

5. Where did the misbehavior take place?

   - In classroom?

   - On playground, hallway, cafeteria, enroute to class?

   - Off school grounds but near school?

6. Is this behavior a common occurrence?

   - For this student?

   - For others in the school?

7. Do you have personal feelings about this student?

   - Have you interacted positively or negatively before this?

   - Do you know this student at all?

8. What are your legal rights when dealing with disruptive students?
   Review the following topics/laws and share with your student teacher:

   - Corporal punishment (state policies)

   - Negligence (parents, guardians, significant adults)

   - Child abuse (emotional, physical, sexual) and how to report it

   - Children with disabilities and the Individuals with Disabilities Act (IDEA)

   - Liability insurance (what is it and who is covered?)

   - Self-defense and excessive force (how are these terms defined?)

   - Search and seizure (drugs, weapons, obscene materials)

   - Copyright laws (Internet, hardcopy) and what is fair use for teaching?

   - First aid and medications (who is responsible for dispensing?)

9. What other issues do you need to think about?

   - _____

   - _____

   - _____

   - _____

   - _____

Common Classroom Problems: How Often Do They Occur?

Discuss the problem areas you deal with on a daily basis. Four categories for misbehaviors are listed in the chart below, with some possible steps to take to deal with each. Add other problem areas that a student teacher might expect. Are these isolated student issues or whole class issues?

Common Problems	*What You Need to Do*
Chronic Work Avoidance Evidenced in being absent regularly, fooling around in class, not passing in assignments, tardiness, etc.	• Make sure the student is capable of work. • Keep accurate records of what is missing. • Talk with the cooperating teacher. • Let the student know how assignments affect grades. • Talk with parents. • Other?
Habitual Rule Breaking Evidenced in calling out in class, not bringing pencil to class regularly, talkative, forgetting other materials, etc.	• Use established consequences. • Try behavior modification systems. • Talk with the student privately. • Discuss the issue with the cooperating teacher. • Talk with parents. • Other?
Hostile Verbal Outbursts Evidenced by angry and loud yelling, chip-on-the-shoulder attitude, defiance when asked to complete assignments, etc.	• See if the outburst is just momentary. • Don't engage in a power struggle. • Remove the student if anger persists. • Talk with the cooperating teacher. • Talk with the principal. • Talk with the guidance counselor. • Talk with parents. • Other?
Fighting, Destruction, Weapons, Alcohol, or Drug Abuse Evidenced in hallway pushing, violent with peers, threats, glazed look in class, etc.	• Send a student for help. • Disperse crowds that may gather to watch. • Calmly talk—do not shout or scream. • Report the incident immediately. • Other?

How to Avoid Common Problems

Review these key areas with your student teacher to avoid discipline problems.

- **Classroom Management:** Have you structured your classroom in an orderly way to avoid potential problems? Traffic flow? Room set-up?

  What could you change to avoid any further issues?

  _____

  _____

  _____

- **Lesson Planning:** Have you designed lessons that meet the needs of all students? Are the lessons challenging but doable? Have you made accommodations for grouping students to avoid potential problems?

  How can you redesign lessons to avoid future discipline problems you are experiencing?

  _____

  _____

  _____

- **Discipline—Rules, Rewards, and Consequences:** Are the rules clearly posted and understood? Do students "own" the rules or are the rules imposed on them? Are you consistent when you apply the consequences? Do you treat all students fairly?

  What do you need to do to be sure your rules, rewards, and consequences are working to avoid problems?

  _____

  _____

  _____

Cases for Discussion and Role-Playing

FOR THE STUDENT TEACHER

These cases will be considered repeat offenses. All of the students have been spoken to at least once.

Case 1. A student shouts out answers during class discussion. She is disruptive by joking and talking to others and writing notes to both boys and girls during the class period.

Case 2. A student sleeps in the back of the room. He is not disruptive, but simply does not do any work or participate in any way.

Case 3. A student is caught cheating during a test and has in the past cheated on homework assignments.

Case 4. Two students are caught fistfighting in the corridor near the classroom about a personal issue from home.

Create your own case study appropriate to your grade level and role-play with your cooperating teacher or invite another student teacher to role-play.

CASE STUDY

_____

_____

_____

_____

_____

_____

_____

_____

Tips for More Effective Disciplining

This brief list describes behaviors effective teachers use to establish optimal learning environments in their classrooms. Check the ones you would like to share with your student teacher.

_____ • Focus on positive behavior when it happens.
Give verbal praise for specific behavior.
Send notes home with students.
Make complimentary phone calls to parents about their child.

_____ • Don't threaten or bribe students to behave.
Students may respond for a short term but will not respect you in the long term, because behavior becomes contingent on continuation of bribe.

_____ • Limit the number of rules you have in the classroom.
Involve students in rule making.
Post consequences for all to see.
Send a copy home to parents to read and sign.
Write rules in a positive way whenever possible.
Make consequences progressive, allowing students to learn from errors.

_____ • Take charge of the classroom in a firm but pleasant manner.
Use your sense of humor to keep students in line.
Communicate your needs honestly to students.
Listen to your students' requests and complaints.

_____ • Give "I"-messages to students instead of "You"-messages.
"I am unhappy with the behavior I am seeing," not "You are misbehaving again."

_____ • Use body language and signals to prevent disruptive behavior.
Make eye contact with the misbehaving student.
Use frown or facial expression.
Walk near the student and lightly tap his or her shoulder.
Use your sense of humor.
Use a cue to have the students look at you (e.g., lights off, raise hands, etc.).

_____ • Don't use sarcasm, cruel remarks, or words to embarrass students.
  No ridicule or intimidation allowed!
  Never touch a student in an abusive way.
  Confrontation in front of a whole class is not recommended.
  If the situation becomes confrontational, remove the student and discuss the problem later.

_____ • Use a variety of teaching strategies to increase student involvement.
  Bored students may find mischief.
  Small groups, partners, and problem solving challenge thinking.
  Change a lesson to prevent a problem.

_____ • Make the best use of materials and resources.
  Audiovisual materials
  Library
  Seating arrangements that prevent problems

_____ • Have a planned discipline strategy.
  Keep records of students who misbehave.
  Gain administrative support when necessary.

_____ • Other tips

  _____

  _____

  _____

  _____

  _____

Problems to Possibilities: Student Conferences and Contracts

Share with your student teacher your ideas for resolving problems with students. A short conference with a student individually or in a small group can make a difference in the ways students respond in class. If you use this strategy, share the idea!

Conference Report

Student's Name: _____ Date: _____

Reason for Conference: _____

_____

Summary of Conference: _____

Signature of Teacher: _____

Signature of Student: _____

You may also want to share a Student Contract to guide the student in changing the behavior.

Student Contract

I state that I will *(change a certain behavior)* _____.

_____ . I will measure my

success by *(how the behavior will be noted as being done)* _____.

For successful demonstration *(I will receive a reward)* _____.

Signed (Teacher): _____ Date: _____

Signed (Student): _____ Date: _____

The contract can also be designed for groups by changing I to we.

When Is It Time to Seek Additional Support?

How do you know you need more help?

_____ When you have exhausted your possibilities

_____ When the student exhibits serious problems beyond the scope of common issues

_____ When your cooperating teacher has determined the student needs additional help

_____ When parents have indicated a need for support

How do you know what kind of help is available for a student?

Talk to...

_____ Special needs teachers

_____ Guidance department

_____ School psychologist/school social worker

_____ Principal

_____ Department chair

_____ School nurse or health department

What should you do?

_____ Maintain accurate records of all misbehaviors with dates of offenses

_____ Write a request for help with your cooperating teacher

How do you know you haven't failed?

_____ You have tried a number of approaches with the student and documented them

_____ Your cooperating teacher has made the decision to refer the student

Cooperating Teacher's Reflection

What have you learned about your own discipline style by sharing your ideas with your student?

JOURNAL ENTRY

Date: _____

_____

_____

_____

_____

_____

_____

REFLECTIVE QUESTIONS

1. What has been the most difficult part of sharing your discipline techniques?

_____

_____

2. How have you seen your student teacher grow in this area?

_____

_____

3. What did you find the most difficult to explain? Why?

_____

_____

Final Reminders and Helpful Hints

_____ Make the punishment fit the crime—running in a hallway should not have a consequence of writing "I will not run." It may turn students off to writing and it doesn't teach them to walk in the hall.

_____ Avoid meaningless writing of sentences as a punishment. Instead, if you require a written explanation, have it be in the form of a letter to you (with proper format), explaining the misbehavior and telling why it won't happen again. Written explanations can be more appropriate than oral ones from two students, especially when they see the situation differently. After reading both letters, the teacher can address the real issue.

_____ Plan private conferences with students who need extra attention, and set goals for improvement. Bring parents in if necessary.

_____ When disciplining, make sure the erring student understands that the teacher doesn't like the behavior—but still likes the student as a person.

_____ Be willing to apologize when you are wrong or make a mistake in judgment when disciplining a student. This will create respect for you among the students.

_____ Sometimes it is appropriate to ignore minor misbehaviors rather than making a major issue out of every situation. Every time you have to stop a class, it inhibits learning for all the students. Select situations carefully to take on in front of the whole class. Private conversations after class may be more productive with some students.

_____ Avoid punishing the whole group for the misbehavior of a few students. Sometimes it is necessary; however, always be ready to explain why you have done it. Parents of good students object to whole-class punishment.

_____ If all else fails, isolate the student who is constantly breaking rules and being disruptive.

_____ Try to catch students being good and compliment them daily!

CHAPTER 13

Assessing, Recording, and Communicating Student Progress

Remember, our task is not to see how our students do on one particular day, but how it's going along the way, ensuring they will be successful whenever the big day comes. We should never be surprised nor should the students.

Vito Perrone

During the practicum, your student teacher will be asked to assess the progress of the students he or she is teaching. Your own system for assessment should be clearly explained before the student teacher is asked to use it. Perhaps you are currently using portfolio assessment, but in the past your school used a traditional report card with letter grades. If you are familiar with other models of assessing and recording student progress besides what you are currently using, familiarize your student teacher with them, as well.

Remember, the student teacher probably has not assessed or recorded a whole classroom before, and it tends to be overwhelming the first time. Many student teachers have reported that this is an area in which they need more guidance. Even though many of them understand the concept of assessment, they do not always have the skill to implement it efficiently.

Assessing and recording students' progress is sometimes a difficult task because of the many differences in ability levels and the time it takes to give thoughtful feedback to each student. You, as the cooperating teacher, are ultimately accountable for the students in your classroom, so work with your student teacher and be aware of what is going on. Don't assume he or she can automatically follow your system the first time! The student teacher may not be aware of the philosophies that guide your assessment procedures, so you need to provide this background information.

If you have shortcuts for correcting papers, reporting grades, designing portfolios, or communicating with parents, tell your student teacher about them. For example, a tip to save time when recording grades is to assign a number to each student in the class that corresponds to A-B-C order of the gradebook. Ask students to place the number in the right-hand corner of each paper passed in. When you collect the papers, put them in numerical order (or have a student do it), and you can quickly record your grades in order. You see who is missing right away. Don't let the student teacher find these tricks out by trial and error. Offer your expertise!

Assessment covers a broad range of topics, from record keeping to reporting student progress to parents. Each area has its own aspects that require different skills. Your student teacher may not be ready to participate in all the aspects of assessment you have established in your classroom. Begin slowly and build on his or her skills.

Part of assessment is keeping accurate records of student progress. One reason for maintaining classroom records is so the teacher can design the curriculum that meets the needs of the students in his or her classroom. The program of study can be made more challenging or broken into small learning experiences if need be. Are there groups of students who need assistance in a particular skill area? Is there an individual student who is significantly growing in a certain skill area? Without accurate record keeping, it would be difficult to keep track of these often subtle patterns. By keeping records, one can assess student progress and focus on what is working and what needs to be worked on.

Another major reason for recording student assessment is to inform the parents of their child's progress. Concrete examples and anecdotal records provide the evidence of where a student is learning. Daily papers, test scores, workbook pages, projects, and other activities provide a reference for student progress. School districts and communities are often interested in how students are doing. Many states also have their own tests for measuring achievement and progress.

The forms, samples, and checklists in this chapter can guide your discussion of assessment. These suggestions are not meant to be all-inclusive, but provide a framework for your discussion. Select those topics that relate to your own procedures, adapt them to meet your needs, and add any topics not covered.

Lesson Plan

Time: Halfway through the practicum

Purpose: To familiarize the student teacher with assessment policies and classroom practices

Objectives:
- To share your assessment and recording systems
- To assist the student teacher in assessing students
- To share alternative systems
- To discuss the role of students' self-evaluation
- To monitor communication between the student teacher and the parents of the students

Materials: Your gradebook, tests, sample student portfolios, etc.

Procedure:
1. Discuss your routine for correcting, assessing, and recording student work on a daily, weekly, and monthly basis.

2. Share other systems of assessment you are aware of and the philosophies behind each one. If you use different systems, explain why.

3. Assist the student teacher in assessing the students.

4. Monitor school-home communication.

5. Reflect on the process for a final discussion.

Other Thoughts/
Notes: Assessment is a complex issue that is ever changing. Make sure the student teacher understands why teachers assess student work. Don't expect him or her to integrate all of these ideas at once or to agree with them all. Assist the student teacher in discovering his or her own assessment philosophy. Use the college to help you define unfamiliar assessment areas.

University Supervisor Suggestions

PLAN: Organize your thoughts and materials, and prepare for your role.

Key Questions

1. What should the student teacher know in regard to classroom assessment and what should he or she be able to do by the end of the practicum?

2. How can the student teacher stay current about state and national initiatives?

Teaching Competency Focus Areas for Chapter 13

Knowledge, Communication, Instructional Practice, Evaluation, Problem Solving, **Equity,** & Professionalism

CONNECT: Use resources to enhance your skills as a supervisor.

People. Who do you know that can assist with assessment issues?

Books and Resources. Rely on portfolio assessment, performance, and outcomes-based topics.

Technology. Connect with Ask Dr. Rubric (www.classnj.org).

ACT: Select the activities that will be useful to you or create your own.

ACTion #1. Survey your student teacher to understand his or her level of competence in assessment.

ACTion #2. Provide support if the student teacher needs more knowledge.

ACTion #3. Encourage self-assessment as a tool for the student teacher.

REFLECT: **Think about your role as a supervisor and write a one-page reflection.**

Choose to respond to the key questions on the previous page, create a prompt of your own, or answer the following question: How can I meet the varying needs of my student teachers in the area of classroom assessment?

How Are Students Assessed and Evaluated?

Share with your student teacher all the types of tests your students will take this year. Review the purposes of the tests and explain the procedures. Explain how all state and local tests relate to the environment for learning you are attempting to create with your students.

STATE TESTING INITIATIVES

Does your state have a statewide testing program? What is its purpose?

Are the students required to pass a high school exit exam? When is it given? What is the test? Are there other state tests required? Which grade levels? Ask to review a copy of the tests if they are at your grade level.

On what standards or frameworks are the tests based? How will this state test affect the curriculum you teach in your classroom?

DISTRICT TESTING PROGRAM

What is the purpose of these tests?

Does the district require tests for certain grades? Note the test names here:

_____

Are these tests similar to the state tests? How?

CLASSROOM ASSESSMENT AND EVALUATION PROCEDURES

How do you use *informal* assessment to assess learning? Journals? Notecards? File folders? Portfolios? Notes in rank book? Share all your strategies with your student teacher.

How do you *formally* assess students for understanding? Teacher-made tests? Publishing company tests? Performance assessment? Portfolios? Share all assessment tools with your student teacher.

Product versus Process

How do you observe student achievement? Will a product let you know that the student achieved the objectives or do you need to observe the student perform and demonstrate the skill or understanding of the topic? Explain the difference between *product* and *process* assessment to your student teacher. Remind him or her that the assessment/evaluation depends on the lesson's objective. Be sure the achievement measure matches the objective designed in the student teacher's lesson plan. Suggestions for product and process assessments include the following:

Product *(paper / pencil)*	*Product* *(visual)*	*Performance Process* *(with or without product)*
Essays	Posters	Oral reports
Book reports	Banners	Speeches
Biographies	Models	Raps
Journals	Diagrams	Dramatizations
Letters	Displays	Debates
Editorials	Videotapes or audiotapes	Songs
Scripts	Portfolios	Poems
Tests	Exhibits	Demonstrations
Research reports	Paintings	Interviews
Short answers	Photos	Skits
Position papers	Websites	News reports

Ask the student teacher to assess his or her own lessons for the following:

Are your lessons always requiring the same type of assessment or evaluation?

Are you providing alternative assessments for all learners?

Assessment and evaluation should include a combination of the following:

Traditional	Teacher-made or standardized tests where there is only one right answer
	Norm- or criterion-referenced tests
	Knowledge and comprehension levels of Bloom's Taxonomy
	Individual's prior knowledge of objectives through pretesting
Open Ended	Guided questions
	Multistep problems
	Higher levels of Bloom's Taxonomy
	Problem-solving approach to thinking
Performance	Hands-on projects and demonstration of skills and understanding
	More than one right answer
	Portfolios
	Creative problem solving through the arts
Informal	Observation of students in groups and individually
	Audiotaping groups and listening later
	Videotaping and viewing later
	Other?

How are the students in your classroom being assessed? How will you explain this information to your student teacher?

Setting Priorities

What should students be able to *do* to show they understand the content/process/skill? Write something? Respond to an open-ended question? Perform a skit? Discuss this question with your student teacher.

Understanding can be demonstrated by observing the student explain, interpret, apply, persuade, create, design, defend, critique, correct, summarize, translate, compare and contrast, and so on, the information or skill into his or her own words.

Ask your student teacher to think about the following questions as he or she plans and assesses:

- What should *all* students be able to know or do at the end of a particular lesson or unit? How will you know if they achieve that goal?

- What would be important for *most* of them to know? How will you know if they do?

- What would be worth knowing for *some* students? How will you know if they do?

Discuss the following questions with your student teacher:

- What should students have a *real understanding* of that will last and carry over?

- What should they be *familiar with* that can be built on in later years?

- What should they have an *awareness level* of that will be built on in later years?

How does a teacher decide the answers to these questions?

Formative and Summative Assessments

FORMATIVE ASSESSMENT IS PRACTICE—IT IS THE DRESS REHEARSAL!

It is authentic, ongoing, sit beside, self-assessing, learn as we go, practice, group work, conversations, checklists, surveys, drill, practice tests, and so on.

• When would you use formative assessments in teaching?

_____

_____

_____

Share this information with your student teacher.

SUMMATIVE ASSESSMENT IS FINAL—IT IS THE OPENING NIGHT OF THE PLAY!

It is the final test, the grade given to an individual student, the final evaluation, the judgment given at the end of the unit or term, the report card grade, the SAT, the final product, a paper test, an artwork project, the final performance, an oral exam, and so on.

• When would you use summative evaluation?

_____

_____

_____

Share this information with your student teacher.

Using Rubrics to Assess Student Learning

Do you use rubrics in your classroom? Rubrics are either holistic or analytical. Holistic scoring values the students' overall thinking and understanding. The score is applied to the overall quality of the task completed. Analytical rubrics award points for each step the students complete in the process. Which type of rubric are you using? Ask your student teacher to create a rubric.

1. What would your list of specific criteria for a good paper, project, or performance in this area be?

_____

_____

_____

2. How could you specifically define degrees of understanding and demonstration?

_____

_____

You can have as many points in your rubric as you find useful—for example:

Accuracy of work in degrees—completely accurate, almost accurate, etc.; few mistakes, many errors; etc.

Clarity—thoughts are clear, hard to understand

Understanding—complete, almost, doesn't understand

Sample Rubric

	Criterion 1	Criterion 2	Criterion 3
3: High understanding			
2: Some understanding			
1: Little understanding			

Record-Keeping Strategies

Teachers use a variety of systems to keep track of student progress. A common way is to use a gradebook. However, many teachers use different systems within their gradebooks. Ask your student teacher to interview several teachers in the building and document the different recording systems.

TEACHER #1: _____

Gradebook System: _____

_____

_____

_____

TEACHER #2: _____

Gradebook System: _____

_____

_____

_____

In addition to using gradebooks, teachers may make anecdotal comments and use journals, index file boxes, or their own plan books to keep track of student progress. Other teachers use checklists or progress charts. Have the student teacher document three other ways to record information and why a teacher might use these systems in addition to a gradebook.

1. _____

2. _____

3. _____

How do you decide if a record-keeping system is effective?

_____ Ask: **Is it easy to use?** (Is it something I will use?)

_____ Ask: **Is it easy to read?** (Can you scan it quickly for information?)

_____ Ask: **Can I derive patterns from it?** (Over time do I see student progress?)

SUGGESTIONS:

_____ Use a highlighter to mark "holes" in your gradebook to scan for missing grades easily.

_____ Use another color highlighter for any grade below average to scan for problem areas quickly.

Ask your student teacher to interview other teachers in the building to see how they document their students' progress.

Portfolio Assessment

Many school districts use an assessment approach called *student portfolios*. This is a system where students collect samples of their work over a period of time and teachers review the skills and progress the student is making by looking at the work. This would be considered a process approach to assessment.

Ask your student teacher to review any college course material that refers to the use of portfolios for student assessment and to share it with you. If you are familiar with the process and are implementing it in your classroom, share that information. Use these questions to guide your student teacher's inquiry.

1. What is portfolio assessment?

_____

_____

2. How is it different from traditional assessment?

_____

_____

3. What are some advantages of portfolio assessment?

_____

_____

4. What are some disadvantages of portfolio assessment?

_____

_____

5. What questions do you have about portfolio assessment?

_____

_____

Student Self-Assessment

How can students monitor their own progress? Share these ideas with your student teacher. Do you use any student self-assessment tools? Do students assess their own learning? If so, how? The following examples here illustrate ways individuals and groups can assess their own progress:

INDIVIDUAL ASSESSMENT OF DAILY WORK

Hard or Easy?

Ask students if they are finding work hard or easy. Make a graph to see how many students are finding things hard or easy.

What Are You Learning?

Take a minute at the end of each class as part of your closing to ask students to write two things they learned in class today. Review these student writings to see how you did as a teacher in presenting your objectives. This exercise can serve two purposes: (1) to see what they recall and (2) to let you know how to plan the next lesson.

More Time?

Have the students vote on whether they think they need more time on the concept you are teaching. Let them reply anonymously on paper or by putting their heads down and raising their hands. Write your own prediction of how the lesson went and what the students will say before reading their responses.

Work Habits

Create a worksheet of statements that the students have to rate from 1 to 5—for example: I worked hard in groups today. I understand the concepts presented.

Teacher Assessment

Create a worksheet about you and your skills in teaching. Rate each from 1 to 5—for example: My teacher presents information in a way I can understand. My teacher listens to my questions. There is time in class for me to practice the skill.

GROUP ASSESSMENT OF DAILY WORK

Create a sheet for cooperating groups to assess their ability to work together and learn the information in a group. They must come to consensus in their rating of each item you create.

Communicating with Students about Their Progress

Teachers use a variety of systems to communicate with their students and keep them on track. The most common formats are the progress slip and the report card, which both go home to parents (see ACT 13-12). Many teachers show progress slips and report cards to students first, before they are sent home. (Remember that progress may include growth in behavior as well as academics.)

In addition to these traditional approaches, teachers are using other procedures to communicate directly with students. Share samples/ideas of any of the following communication systems you are familiar with or have used:

_____ 1. **Student Mailboxes/Teacher Mailbox.** Teachers and students can leave notes for one another about assignments, papers due, make-up work, and so on.

_____ 2. **Student Conference.** The teacher establishes a schedule and meets with individual students privately about their progress. All students meet with the teacher, not just the failing students.

_____ 3. **Progress Chart.** A subject-related progress chart is given to each student that visually documents the number of assignments completed, scores, projects, and so on.

_____ 4. **Warnings.** When in danger of failing, a student receives a "red" note.

_____ 5. **Compliments.** The student receives written or verbal acknowledgment of quality work.

_____ 6. **Checklist.** Place checklists inside daily or weekly folders. The students can see what has been checked by you and approved for credit.

_____ 7. **Progress List.** Secondary students may be instructed to maintain their own grades.

_____ **8. Midterm Progress Reports.** These list completed assignments and suggestions for improvement.

_____ **9. Other ideas:**

_____

_____

_____

_____

_____

_____

_____

_____

_____

_____

Communicating with Parents

Teachers communicate with parents for many reasons, including how their child interacts with other students, how the child behaves in class, and/or what the academic progress of the student is at the time of the conversation. Student teachers need to be aware of the variety of ways to communicate this information. Some common procedures include the following:

_____ 1. **Telephone Call Conferences** (Suggestion: Send a note home telling parents what time you will be calling)

  • To compliment students

  • To give warnings

_____ 2. **Written Communication**

  • Informal notes to parents

  • Formal progress slips from school office/midterm reports

  • Formal progress slips/behavior checklists (teacher designed)

  • Daily homework sheets initialed by teacher and sent home

_____ 3. **Meetings**

  • Informal

  • Regarding a particular issue

  • Formal (regular basis for a particular student, including other teachers, principal, guidance, etc.)

  • Parent conference (appointments for parents on a certain day)

_____ 4. **Report Cards**

  • Delivered by students

  • Picked up by parents

_____ 5. **Group Meetings with Parents**

  • Open house evening

  • Special event in your classroom

_____ 6. **Your Ideas** _____

_____

Cooperating Teacher's Reflection

What is the most important thing I think my student teacher should understand about assessment?

JOURNAL ENTRY

Date: _____

_____

_____

_____

_____

_____

_____

REFLECTIVE QUESTIONS

1. What has been the most difficult part of the discussion about assessment?

_____

_____

2. What have I learned from my student teacher about assessment?

_____

_____

3. How has this conversation helped me as a teacher?

_____

_____

Final Reminders and Helpful Hints

_____ In addition to portfolio assessment, other alternative methods include using videotapes or having students demonstrate skills through performances. Have the student teacher investigate these if there is interest in alternative methods.

_____ Assessing, record keeping, and communicating are an overwhelming part of a teacher's professional life. Teachers rarely have an opportunity to share these procedures with each other, so use this as an opportunity to discover new systems for yourself, too.

_____ Let the student teacher know assessment is a process that can be cumbersome and overwhelming. Guide him or her in selecting a few procedures to practice instead of trying them all. There will be time in the future to change strategies. Awareness of strategies is most important now.

_____ Simplify the process whenever possible and share it in an organized way to avoid any misunderstandings.

_____ Invite the student teacher to design his or her own procedure. You may be pleasantly surprised!

_____ List your reminders below:

_____ _____

_____ _____

_____ _____

_____ _____

Culminating the Student Teaching Experience

The three chapters in this section are Other Important Issues, Final Evaluation Procedures, and Completing the Experience. Chapter 14 discusses topics that may not specifically involve teaching but relate to the professional aspects of being a teacher. Guidelines, special policies, and issues that relate to substitute teaching should be addressed before the student teacher completes the practicum.

Evaluation procedures should be kept separate from completion activities, as they are in this handbook. Student teachers are usually evaluated by the college supervisor with input from the cooperating teacher. This evaluation becomes part of the student teacher's record and grade-point average. The completion activities you organize involve the recognition of the relationships that have been created during the experience.

Use this section to culminate the student teacher experience. Add any other topics that are needed to prepare your student teacher for his or her first classroom.

CHAPTER 14

Other Important Issues

A mind that is stretched by a new experience can never go back to its old dimensions.
Oliver Wendell Holmes

Before the student teacher completes the practicum, you should briefly cover as many of the following issues in this chapter as possible. Some of them relate directly to the practicum; others will be useful when the student is hired as a first-year teacher. You may have other issues that are not included in this chapter. Feel free to add them and provide the information to your student teacher.

The forms, samples, and checklists will help you make your student teacher aware of various aspects of the teaching profession.

Lesson Plan

Time: Nearing the end of the practicum

Purpose: To review any other issues that relate to the practicum or to the first year of teaching

Objectives:
- To review practicum-related issues
- To review professional issues

Materials: School documents

Procedure:
1. Share personal information with the student teacher.
2. Invite others to speak with the student teacher.
3. Reflect on and review any other issues.

Other Thoughts/ Notes: For whatever reason, some important issues simply don't come up and thus are never discussed. If a student teacher has a spring practicum, special education referrals may have already been done in the fall. Many issues relate to seasonal routines and should still be discussed, regardless of whether they fall in the student teacher's practicum time. Keep a notebook of these stray issues and inform the student teacher about them when the time is right.

University Supervisor Suggestions

PLAN: Organize your thoughts and materials, and prepare for your role.

Key Questions

1. How will the student teacher learn about the other issues in this chapter?

2. How can I enhance the student teacher's experience with current information?

Teaching Competency Focus Areas for Chapter 14

Knowledge, Communication, Instructional Practice, Evaluation, Problem Solving, Equity, & **Professionalism**

CONNECT: Use resources to enhance your skills as a supervisor.

People. Try career centers, teachers' unions, professional organizations, and so on.

Books and Resources. A wealth of information is in the library!

Technology. Go on line to check state and national teachers groups and organizations.

ACT: Select the activities that will be useful to you or create your own.

ACTion #1. Assist the student teacher in getting accurate information about substituting.

ACTion #2. Discuss special education laws and issues as they relate to this setting.

ACTion #3. Share your networks and information resources.

REFLECT: **Think about your role as a supervisor and write a one-page reflection.**

Choose to respond to the key questions on the previous page, create a prompt of your own, or answer the following question: How can I support my student teacher in learning about all aspects of the professional life of a teacher?

Policies for Substitute Teaching

Substitute teaching refers to instruction of another class in the school. Taking over the cooperating teacher's class for a day when the teacher is ill or on professional business is not officially substituting, because, in theory, this is also the student teacher's classroom.

When other teachers in the building are ill, principals have been known to use a student teacher to substitute if that student is near the end of the practicum. It can be a rewarding experience for a student teacher who is ready for a new experience. On the other hand, it can be a frustrating experience for both of you if you have to teach the lessons the student teacher was supposed to teach, and if the student teacher is unfamiliar with the routine of another class.

In some schools, cooperating teachers take the other class instead of having the student teacher do it. This, of course, would be a voluntary activity for the cooperating teacher. The following questions will guide you in dealing with the issues that arise when student teachers become substitutes.

_____ 1. Review the college handbook for any policies regarding student teachers and substituting. There are often recommendations not to substitute unless there is an emergency situation and the principal requests this assistance.

_____ 2. Talk with the college supervisor about this issue to get input in case you have to make a recommendation to the principal about the ability of the student teacher to substitute.

_____ 3. Discuss the possibility of substituting in emergency situations and get a feeling for whether your student teacher is comfortable to do this if asked.

_____ 4. Talk with the building principal to find out the principal's intention regarding substituting and how it might be implemented with this student teacher. Share your feelings about the readiness of this student teacher to leave your supervision.

_____ 5. Talk with other teachers to see how they feel about this issue.

_____ 6. Think about your own perceptions and the benefits and weaknesses of having your student teacher substitute in your school.

243

_____ 7. Issues of payment need to be discussed before any substituting takes place (normally practicum students are not paid for emergency substituting).

_____ 8. After the practicum is complete, your student teacher can be added to the substitute list (with your recommendation) and receive payment with no questions.

_____ 9. District policies for substitute teaching:

_____

_____

_____

_____

_____

Legal Issues

Practicum students need to be aware of key issues that relate to their student teaching and their work in schools as future teachers.

_____ 1. Responsibility during supervisory duties (e.g., cafeteria, hall duty, bus duty, playground supervision)

- If there is a problem (accident, fight, etc.), you and your principal should explain what the student teacher should do if he or she is alone at these duties. Also, what are the practicum student's rights as a student teacher? Who is responsible? Can the student teacher ever be blamed for any incident?

- To prevent problems, good supervisory practices should always be in effect (i.e., walking around playgrounds, staying alert to the activities of groups, and not just talking to one student when on a duty).

- The cooperating teacher should remain with the student teacher on all duties until full-time teaching is started and even then if needed.

_____ 2. Responsibility to report neglect or abuse of students, with students in your classroom or other classes.

- Student teachers need to be aware of any legal policies that require them to report any suspected cases of child abuse. The student teacher should report these to you and you can take proper action.

_____ 3. List other legal issues:

_____

_____

_____

_____

_____

Guidelines for Referring Students

During the course of a school year, a teacher may have difficulty with a student and, in spite of all efforts to assist this student, may need additional support for academic or emotional reasons. To obtain support, teachers usually have to fill out forms, keep anecdotal records, meet with parents, and provide specific recommendations. Student teachers may not be aware of this process because it often happens in meetings outside of the classroom when the teacher is not teaching.

Even if you are not in the process of referring a student, it is an important area that needs to be discussed. Many beginning teachers are unaware of the process and need guidance in knowing when they should refer a student.

_____ 1. Show the student teacher the school forms used to refer a student for special services.

_____ 2. If there are any state guidelines, put together a packet the student teacher can refer to at a later time. The special education director can help prepare this information.

_____ 3. If you have any federal programs in your school, make the student teacher aware of them. If there are Chapter 1 teachers working in the district, let the student teacher talk directly with them.

Discuss the following:

• How do you know when it is time to refer a student?

_____

_____

_____

_____

_____

_____

- List examples of students who have been referred in the past.

_____

_____

_____

_____

_____

_____

- What should be done before any referral process takes place?

_____

_____

_____

_____

_____

_____

Including Students with Special Needs

Rather than making outside placements or "pulling" students with specials needs for related services, classroom teachers work collaboratively with special education teachers. Some of the models include coteaching; others include coplanning or support.

Discuss with your student teacher the issues related to this type of collaboration (inclusion). The following questions may guide your discussion:

_____ Why is your school/district using this model?

_____ How does it differ from the "pull-out" referral model?

_____ Can both models exist in a district/school? How?

_____ What is the philosophy/theory behind the inclusion model?

_____ What are the benefits to this type of inclusion vs. pulling students out?

_____ What are some drawbacks?

_____ How is coteaching part of the model?

_____ What are the benefits for coteachers?

_____ Other issues: _____

_____

_____

_____

_____

_____

_____

Professional Development

An important part of being a competent teacher is ongoing professional development. Share with your student teacher how you and your colleagues at your school stay current in the field of education.

_____ 1. Books, magazines, articles you are reading

_____

_____

_____ 2. Workshops you have attended

_____

_____

_____ 3. Associations and teacher networks to which you belong

_____

_____

_____ 4. School district programs/faculty meetings/in-service

_____

_____

_____ 5. Teacher union membership/leadership roles

_____

_____

_____ 6. College courses/ advanced degrees

_____

_____

_____ 7. Special training you have received

_____

_____

_____ 8. Presentations/workshops you have conducted

_____

_____

_____ 9. Other professional experiences/trips/grants/awards

_____

_____

_____ 10. Other professional issues for discussion:

_____

_____

Teachers' Unions and Professional Associations

1. Share your perspective of teachers' unions and teachers' associations. Explain why you have this point of view. List some key points here that you need to address.

_____

_____

_____

_____

2. Encourage your student teacher to talk with other teachers in the building who have a different point of view. List possible teachers' names here.

_____

_____

_____

_____

3. Set up a meeting with a union representative so your student teacher can gather information about the union. Have the representative discuss local, state, and national unions. List name, date, and time of meeting here.

_____

_____

_____

_____

4. Discuss the differences between a teachers' union and a professional association. List key points here.

_____

_____

_____

_____

_____

_____

Cooperating Teacher's Reflection

How do these other issues affect my life as a teacher?

JOURNAL ENTRY

Date: _____

_____

_____

_____

_____

REFLECTIVE QUESTIONS

1. Which issue stands out for me as a focus of my teaching this year? Why?

_____

_____

2. What are some other issues I should discuss before my student leaves?

_____

_____

3. How can my own professional development assist me in handling these issues?

_____

_____

Final Reminders and Helpful Hints

_____ These areas affect a teacher's life in the classroom, yet many of them are outside the daily routine of actually teaching students. They are important because the way in which any of them is handled can affect the daily teaching of the students.

_____ Policies, legal issues, and any type of guidelines a teacher needs to know should be shared during the practicum. Many student teachers just see the four walls of a classroom and then are shocked to learn how many other issues relate to their teaching.

_____ Collaboration with other adults through special education teams offers new opportunities to student teachers as they enter the world of teaching. If there are any other teacher–teacher collaborations in your school, share that information.

_____ Professional development is the key to remaining current in the profession. Encourage the student teacher to begin now by participating with you at school-related programs and in-service.

_____ List your reminders below:

_____

_____

_____

_____

_____

_____

_____

CHAPTER 15

Final Evaluation Procedures

Remember, evaluation is not the end but the beginning of the reflective process.

Lee Teitel

The final evaluation usually occurs during the final week of student teaching when you meet with the student teacher and the college supervisor to discuss the overall teaching progress. The information at the final meeting should be a summary of the student teacher's progress and should include a synthesis of the feedback you have been giving to your student teacher throughout the whole experience. Review all the materials you have collected during the practicum to highlight the growth areas. Remember: The student teacher is not a finished product but optimally a lifelong learner, and this final evaluation does not mean he or she is now "magically" a teacher. Look for growth and potential. The final evaluation usually involves:

- A grade from the college supervisor

- Your signature on a final form that relates to certification

- A recommendation you may be asked to write for your student teacher

Check with the college supervisor to see how your input will be used for the grade the student teacher is given and if there are any other final duties you need to complete. The final evaluation is a time to reflect on the whole experience and think about what worked well and what you might do differently next time. At this time, you also may want to participate in the following:

- A self-evaluation about the experience

- Feedback to the college supervisor about the practicum process

- Feedback from your student teacher about your skills as a cooperating teacher and the college supervisor's skills as a supervisor

You can use this reflective process to discover what you have learned about yourself as a teacher and to find out what your student teacher's perceptions were about your skills as a teacher educator.

The forms, samples, and checklists in this chapter provide a framework for the final evaluation process.

Lesson Plan

Time: The last two weeks

Title: Final Evaluation

Purpose: To summarize the experience by reviewing the progress of the student teacher throughout the practicum

Objectives:
- To review the goals established at the beginning of the practicum
- To reread observation and feedback forms
- To collaborate with the college supervisor regarding the final grade
- To write a recommendation for the student teacher

Procedure:
1. Review materials and write down the qualities of the student teacher.
2. Meet with both the student teacher and the college supervisor.
3. Write your recommendation.
4. Ask for feedback from the student teacher.
5. Provide feedback to the college supervisor.
6. Reflect on the experience.

**Other Thoughts/
Notes:** The final evaluation is an important time for the student teacher. It may be very emotional, depending on the quality of the experience. Keep the supervisor aware of any issues that need to be addressed *before* the final meeting so that there are no surprises when you meet as a group.

University Supervisor Suggestions

PLAN: Organize your thoughts and materials, and prepare for your role.

Key Questions

1. What needs to be completed for the final close-out meeting?

2. How will you complete final written evaluations for each student teacher?

Teaching Competency Focus Areas for Chapter 15

Knowledge, Communication, Instructional Practice, **Evaluation,** Problem Solving, Equity, & **Professionalism**

CONNECT: Use resources to enhance your skills as a supervisor.

People. Review progress with cooperating teacher(s) and other site professionals.

Books and Resources. Use college guidelines and handbooks to complete requirements.

Technology. Use the computer to type reports and maintain a file.

ACT: Select the activities that will be useful to you or create your own.

ACTion #1. Set a meeting time with the student teacher to check all paperwork and requirements.

ACTion #2. Write your final evaluation based on teaching competencies.

ACTion #3. Ask your supervisor to review any problematic evaluation reports.

REFLECT: Think about your role as a supervisor and write a one-page reflection.

Choose to respond to the key questions on the previous page, create a prompt of your own, or answer the following question: How can I complete final evaluations in a systematic, organized way?

Final Evaluation: The Summative Report

This final summative report is completed by college supervisors to assess the student teacher's progress. You are an integral part of this process and need to give your input to the college supervisor. Your student teacher should follow these steps to self-assess:

STEP ONE: COMPLETION OF REQUIREMENTS

Review the syllabus requirements and check for completeness. Ask yourself: Did I do everything I was asked to do?

_____ Text and readings

_____ Observation forms

_____ Products that need to be complete (e.g., samples of lesson plans, units, teaching binder, etc.)

_____ College-related requirements (e.g., attendance on campus for seminars or other required events)

_____ Journals with weekly entry

_____ Other requirements _____

_____ Any extra credit completed during the semester (included in teaching binder or portfolio)

Did you complete all requirements on time and present them clearly and free of error?

STEP TWO: COMPETENCE IN FIELD EXPERIENCE AND RELATED REQUIREMENTS

Review your field experience for evidence of competence. Ask yourself: How do I match up with criteria established at the beginning of the semester?

_____ Subject-mater knowledge

_____ Communication

_____ Instructional practice

_____ Evaluation

_____ Problem solving

_____ Equity

_____ Professionalism

      Review all forms completed throughout the semester:

_____ Initial visit

_____ Midterm

_____ Final observation

_____ Other informal verbal feedback you noted

_____ Other written feedback

      Review your journal entries, audiotapes, and videotapes. Did you demonstrate a beginning level of competence in all areas?

STEP THREE: DOCUMENTING SCHOOL OF EDUCATION THEMES

Ask yourself: Was I required to demonstrate evidence of the School of Education themes?

      (Sample themes: Promoting Social Justice, Constructing Knowledge, Inquiring into Practice, Accommodating Diversity, Collaborating with Others, etc.) Where did you demonstrate them? How would your supervisor know?

STEP FOUR: COMPARE YOUR SELF-ASSESSMENT WITH UNIVERSITY SUPERVISOR AND COOPERATING TEACHER

Meet with the college supervisor at your Close Out Meeting and compare your self-assessment with the evaluation the supervisor has prepared. Be sure to bring all completed requirements and student teaching binder for final review. The supervisor will now be ready to complete the Summative Report.

Typically, grades are assigned by the college supervisor with input from the cooperating teacher. Since there are many college requirements, the supervisor must take responsibility for compiling all information and recommending the final grade. Final grades for student teachers are then submitted to the Director of Practicum or Field Experiences and forwarded to the registrar for placement on the transcript.

The Final Summative Report consists of the grade and a short narrative to support the grade. The narrative usually uses the certification competencies as a format. The cooperating teacher will also write a letter of recommendation for certification to be placed in your file at the college.

Optional Job Recommendation Letter

Student teachers often ask supervisors and cooperating teachers to write letters of recommendation for the job search. If you feel your final summative report is acceptable, the letters of recommendation can serve two purposes: (1) completion of student teaching and (2) job search recommendation. If you require another format, give your supervisor and cooperating teacher several weeks to complete these letters.

Final Meeting with the Supervisor

It is important to have all your notes and observations together before the final three-way meeting with the college supervisor and the student teacher. If any questions arise, you will have the materials to support your position.

_____ Review the goals set at the initial meeting. Did the student teacher meet the goals?

_____ Review the requirements set by the college or by you. Are all the required activities complete?

_____ Review your observation notes and summarize them. How would you rate your observations of your student teacher?

_____ Review your student teacher's competence in the following areas that apply:

• Lesson planning

• Individual differences

• Classroom management and daily routine tasks

• Discipline techniques

• Assessment and reporting student progress

• Teaching strategies

• Knowledge of content/curriculum

• Use of technology and/or audiovisual resources

• Interaction with parents/community/staff/faculty

• Special activities, field trips, etc.

• Student teacher's interest in professional activities/reading

• Student teacher's extracurricular activities

_____ Review other information that relates to the experience.

_____ Provide input into the grade the college will be awarding the student teacher.

Note: Cooperating teachers usually have to sign the certification paperwork for state license and write a recommendation.

Cooperating Teacher's Recommendation for Certification

As part of some state certification procedures, the cooperating teacher is often required to write a letter of recommendation that states the competence of the student teacher. (The student teacher may use this for the job search, too.)

This letter should consist of the following:

- The statement that recommends the student teacher for state certification
- Example(s) of work done that demonstrates teaching competencies
- The date and semester the student taught
- A brief description of the school and type of classroom(s) in which he or she worked
- Reasons you think he or she would be a good teacher

SUGGESTIONS FOR YOUR LETTER

_____ 1. Use school or personal letterhead if possible.

_____ 2. Type your letter and have a colleague proofread for errors.

_____ 3. Write the in third person, past tense, avoiding excessive use of the word *I*.

_____ 4. If you have to put the letter on a certain form and it is too small, ask if you can attach your letter to the form and say "See attached."

_____ 5. Describe the setting—that is, grade, subject, school, length of practicum, student population—and include any unusual facts about the teaching situation.

_____ 6. Identify yourself in the letter as a classroom teacher with x number of years of experience. Use your experience as a teacher and cooperating teacher to provide the basis of verifying what you will say in the letter.

_____ 7. Use the following to guide your comments in the recommendation:

- Your own school evaluation instrument

- Certification standards

- The qualities of your student teacher:

    Attitude toward teaching

    Oral communication skills

    Written communication skills

    Ability to reflect

    Productivity/creativity

    Motivation

    Enthusiasm

    Dependability

    Appearance

- Kinds of experiences: small group, large group, centers, projects, etc.

- Instructional management: planning skills, organization, ability to relate to diverse needs

- Behavioral management: classroom management and discipline skills

- Working relationship: students, parents, you, other staff members, principal

_____ 8. Refer to an outstanding achievement the student teacher had during the practicum.

_____ 9. Be specific about your student teacher's skills and qualities, especially if you would like him or her to stand out in a pile of applications. All letters tend to look alike. A personal anecdote or description often stays in a principal's mind. Prospective employers who read through letters are looking for anecdotal or documentary evidence that actually occurred during student teaching. They would like to hire a person who can uniquely contribute to their school.

_____ 10. Be honest and fair to the student teacher. Give strengths and weaknesses, being careful not to overdo either one. If you do not have many good things to say about the student teacher, you may want to share that before you write the recommendation. The student teacher may then decide not to use you as a reference.

Sample Recommendation Letter for an Outstanding Student Teacher

Ms. _____ very successfully completed her practicum experience at the _____ High School in Anytown, USA. She spent 14 weeks observing, assisting, and teaching in my English class. Our school is noted for a diverse student population and two of our classes are heterogeneously grouped, which offers a challenge to even our most experienced teachers.

Ms. _____'s warm personality and rapport with the students were excellent. Her knowledge of the subject was even noticed by many faculty members in our department. Her willingness to take suggestions, modify lessons, and experiment with new strategies demonstrated her motivation and reflection about teaching and learning.

She was able to communicate effectively and she displayed many fine personal and professional qualities normally attributed to outstanding teachers. She carried out her responsibilities in a responsible and dependable manner and consistently asked to participate in after-school activities and teacher events.

During the practicum, Ms. _____ took responsibility for three classes and assumed the duties of planning and teaching an entire unit. Because of her creativity and enthusiasm for the subject, students responded positively to her lessons. Her students' grades in the areas she presented were well above satisfactory. Her ability to manage a daily routine and the classroom discipline that relates to that was exemplary.

In my opinion as a classroom teacher for 21 years who has prepared more than seven student teachers, Ms._____ is an excellent candidate for your school. She has tremendous initiative, a desire to continue to learn, and a reflective practitioner outlook. Along with her command of the subject area and her effective teaching strategies with adolescents, she is a model of an excellent teacher. I would strongly encourage you to interview and to give serious consideration to this prospective teacher. She would be an asset to any English department.

Sincerely,

Sample Recommendation Letter for a Professionally Competent Student Teacher

Mr. _____ taught in the fifth grade at the _____ School in Anytown, USA, during the fall semester 1999. I served as the cooperating teacher during this practicum experience for the 14 weeks and have been a classroom teacher for 18 years in this system. My experience as a cooperating teacher includes other colleges as well as _____ _____.

Mr. _____ had a positive, successful experience in my classroom. He performed all of his teaching duties in a responsible and dependable manner. I particularly was impressed with his strengths in relating to the students. He planned his lessons well and was sensitive to the needs of the students. His growth in all areas was apparent from the first week to the final meeting.

Mr. _____ has the potential to become an effective teacher. His dependability, planning skills, and communication with students are all part of his strengths. I can predict Mr. _____ will become an effective classroom teacher with the proper guidance from a teacher mentor or the building principal.

If you would like any further information, feel free to contact me.

Sincerely,

Sample Recommendation Letter after an Unsuccessful Experience

Ms._____ has just completed 15 weeks of student teaching in my first-grade classroom. Throughout the experience she has strengthened her knowledge of developmental practice in early childhood education. She has achieved the ability to recognize excellence, remediate weaknesses, and foster mutual respect among students.

However, her ability to plan lessons and submit daily routine information on time was not as successful. In spite of a warm and creative personality, Ms._____ frequently used inappropriate information in class that showed a lack of achievement in the content area.

With careful supervision and the proper guidance from a teacher mentor or the building principal, Ms. _____ _____ could become a good teacher.

Sincerely,

Providing Feedback to the College Supervisor

1. Share any information you have with the college supervisor regarding the following:

   _____ Information you received from the college before you began experience

   _____ Three-way conferences: initial, midterm, final

   _____ The student teacher handbook

   _____ Your role as a teacher educator

   _____ Questions you may have

2. List your compliments for the supervisor regarding the program.

   _____

   _____

3. List any suggestions you have for the program.

   _____

   _____

4. Would you like another student teacher? Let the supervisor know.

   Note: You may also want to give advice to any teachers who are planning to become cooperating teachers. Share what you have learned!

Feedback from Your Student Teacher

After the grading and final conference are complete, you may want to ask your student teacher for some information regarding your role. It should not interfere with or be part of the final evaluation; rather, it is a way for you personally to discover how the student teacher perceives you as a cooperating teacher. Use the ideas to assist you in future experiences.

The student teacher may answer any of the following questions and then make up three more to answer.

1. What was the most important thing I did for you during the practicum?

_____

_____

_____

2. What did you find least valuable in my supervision?

_____

_____

_____

3. What should I be sure to do again with a future student teacher?

_____

_____

_____

4. Describe my style of supervision.

_____

_____

_____

5. What do you wish I had done during the practicum?

_____

_____

_____

6. _____

_____

_____

7. _____

_____

_____

8. _____

_____

_____

Cooperating Teacher's Reflection

How does the process of evaluating your student teacher impact your experience as a supervisor and coach?

JOURNAL ENTRY

Date: _____

_____

_____

_____

_____

REFLECTIVE QUESTIONS

1. What was the most difficult part of evaluating your student teacher?

_____

_____

2. Did you give feedback to the college supervisor? Why or why not?

_____

_____

3. Did you ask your student teacher to give you feedback? Why or why not?

_____

_____

4. What did you learn about evaluation in general by participating in this process?

_____

_____

Final Reminders and Helpful Hints

_____ Remind yourself that the student teacher does not have to be a "perfect" teacher at the end of the student teaching experience. You should see growth and development over the course of time, and that is part of the evaluation.

_____ Keep all your written comments, notes, and documentation in one place for easy access if you need to validate any comment you make on an evaluation or recommendation.

_____ Ask whether the student teacher would like feedback from the classroom students at the end of the experience. Students are often quite honest and may even give very good suggestions. Design a form together that is appropriate to the grade level and distribute to the students if the student teacher would like this information.

_____ Discuss the whole process of evaluation with your student teacher. Share your personal feelings about the evaluation process.

_____ Encourage your student teacher to write a self-evaluation that summarizes the whole experience of the practicum.

_____ Write a self-evaluation about your role as a cooperating teacher.

_____ Share your self-evaluations if both of you are willing.

_____ Write your final reminders here for your next experience:

_____

_____

_____

_____

_____

_____

_____

CHAPTER 16

Completing the Experience

Stay in touch with your student teacher after the practicum if you want to offer ongoing support to a beginning teacher.

Madeline Davern

After the final evaluation is finished, many student teachers and cooperating teachers think the experience is over. However, the practicum experience is much more than the evaluation, observations, and details of teaching. It is also about building relationships. Student teachers often bond with individual students or whole classes, and they need to complete the relationship formally with the students.

You may even find you have an emotional reaction to your student teacher leaving the classroom. Even if the student teacher is not the most outstanding teacher in your view, you may find you have an attachment that goes beyond the routine supervision. After all, you have shared the intimacy of your classroom, your students, and your ideas with this prospective teacher.

Some student teachers are very emotional about leaving the classroom, and you need to be sensitive to this. Providing a culminating student teaching event or a formal way the students can say good-bye often alleviates the emotional tension of leaving.

Some cooperating teachers prefer to coteach with the student teacher the last week so the students see both teachers again as they did in the beginning. This means the student teacher must do his or her full-time teaching the weeks before the final week. It allows the students in the class to get used to their own teacher again and provides time for the student teacher to clean up and return materials borrowed during the semester.

The four main areas to consider during the completion of the student teaching experience are:

1. A final activity with students

2. The final collecting of information for your portfolio

3. A final communication from you

4. Discussion about your relationship in the future

The forms, samples, and checklists in this chapter will assist you in communicating with your student teacher in these four areas.

Lesson Plan

Time: The final week of the practicum

Title: Completing the Practicum

Purpose: To provide an opportunity for completing the experience with the students, school, and you, the cooperating teacher

Objectives:
- To design a culminating activity with the students
- To encourage the student teacher to prepare an activity
- To write the final letter to the student teacher
- To complete relationships in a positive way
- To discuss your future relationship
- To assist the student teacher in designing his or her presentation portfolio

Procedure:
1. Discuss the completion process with the student teacher and make decisions.
2. Plan a surprise event.
3. Exchange completion letters with each other.
4. Design the portfolio with the student teacher.
5. Discuss your future relationship.
6. Reflect on the whole experience.

**Other Thoughts/
Notes:** Make the completion process comfortable. It doesn't matter if the student teacher was effective or ineffective; you still have to break the bond and the relationships with the students in a healthy way. If you need advice, talk with a colleague or the college supervisor. The student teaching experience is one the practicum student will remember forever. Make the completion a celebration of learning and growing.

University Supervisor Suggestions

PLAN: **Organize your thoughts and materials, and prepare for your role.**

Key Questions

1. How will I suggest the student teacher leave his or her school settings?

2. What will I expect the student teacher to give me as a product?

Teaching Competency Focus Areas for Chapter 16

Knowledge, Communication, Instructional Practice, **Evaluation,** Problem Solving, Equity, & **Professionalism**

CONNECT: **Use resources to enhance your skills as a supervisor.**

People. Send thank you notes to all who participated in assisting the student teacher.

Books and Resources. Read *Tips from the Trenches* by Chase and Chase.

Technology. Education Station on the Internet.

ACT: **Select the activities that will be useful to you or create your own.**

ACTion #1. Provide your student teacher with a variety of completion activities.

ACTion #2. Complete with each student privately and acknowledge his or her work.

ACTion #3. Be available for any last-minute issues that arise from evaluation reports.

> **REFLECT:** **Think about your role as a supervisor and write a one-page reflection.**

Choose to respond to the key questions on the previous page, create a prompt of your own, or answer the following question: How do I complete with the schools and cooperating professionals at the sites?

Possible Closing Activities

STUDENT CENTERED

_____ Student-made class book and with messages to the student teacher—may include photographs or drawings

_____ Videotape of students talking to the student teacher

_____ Going-away gift with small school supplies (each student can bring in one item) supplies can be put in a basket or in a carpenter's apron that says "Super Teacher"

_____ Class poem or limerick that relates to the student teacher

_____ Class newspaper or magazine headline that features the student teacher and the lessons taught throughout the practicum

_____ Your ideas:

_____ _____

_____ _____

SCHOOL CENTERED

_____ Faculty breakfast at which student teacher is acknowledged

_____ Presentation sharing accomplishments of student teacher at department meeting or faculty meeting

_____ Principal's award to the student teacher in the weekly bulletin

_____ Article in the school newspaper saying good-bye

_____ Your ideas:

_____ _____

_____ _____

COMMUNITY CENTERED

_____ Article for the local newspaper about your student teacher

_____ An event hosted by the parent teacher group to honor the student teacher

_____ Your ideas:

_____   _____

_____   _____

Designing a Presentation Portfolio (for the Student Teacher)

MY PHILOSOPHY

1. Three words that describe me as a teacher:

   • _____

   • _____

   • _____

2. Three phrases that relate to my beliefs about teaching:

   • I believe _____

   • I believe _____

   • I believe _____

Use these to write a one-page philosophy of education. You may also include goals for yourself as a beginning teacher.

After writing your philosophy, select three or four lessons you taught during the practicum that demonstrate your philosophy. Describe each lesson and tell how the students learned.

Place your philosophy and your lessons in a notebook or portfolio case to share at a job interview. You may want to audiotape your philosophy and send it along with your cover letter and resumé to encourage a principal to call you for an interview. It would allow your voice to be heard and also make you a bit different from other candidates.

In addition to your philosophy, you should consider including the following in your portfolio:

_____ • Reflections about your teaching

_____ • Photographs of students participating in your classroom

_____ • An audiotape or videotape

_____ • Examples of earlier prepracticum projects

Planning a Surprise Celebration

Depending on the size and scope of your celebration, you may also want to add the element of surprise. Students of all ages like to keep secrets, and the student teachers are often unsuspecting victims of these fun celebrations.

TO KEEP A SECRET, YOU HAVE TO BE VERY ORGANIZED

_____ 1. When the student teacher leaves the room, tell the students about your idea to plan a surprise. Set the date and the time for the event. Pick a time when the student teacher will have to be out of the room for the period before so the students can decorate. Make a flyer to go home if you are asking students to bring in a gift.

_____ 2. Ask the students what they would like to give the student teacher (e.g., card, book, video, etc.). Select two students to be in charge and to pass the book or card around the room without getting caught by the student teacher! The students could also make individual cards.

_____ 3. If you decide to have food, set up a refreshment committee. Buy paper products and appoint a clean-up committee.

_____ 4. Select a decoration committee that can make a banner that everyone can autograph.

_____ 5. Take photographs of all the students and put them in a book. Students can autograph under their photo with a special message about what they learned from the student teacher.

_____ 6. Prepare everything a week in advance to make sure it will be complete on the day of the event.

_____ 7. On the day of the event, have the student teacher called out of the room by the office so the students can set everything up.

_____ 8. Call the student teacher back when everything is ready and yell SURPRISE!

Student Teacher Good-Byes

Very often, a student teacher establishes a bond with one or more students. The student teacher may want to write these individuals a final note to let the students know how much they meant to him or her. Especially with primary students there is a real feeling of "loss" if the student teacher worked with a child in a special helping way. You might need to coach the student teacher in separating in a healthy way so no student in your class feels abandoned.

The class will also miss the student teacher as much as the student teacher will miss them. The student teacher may want to write a good-bye letter to the whole class. One clever student teacher even wrote a good-bye poem that included every single child's name in it! Some student teachers give the class a gift for the classroom, such as a book, a plant, or school supplies.

SAMPLE LETTER FOR ELEMENTARY STUDENTS

Dear Students,

Saying good-bye is never easy. It has been very hard for me to think about leaving your classroom. From the very first moment I came into your room, I knew I would love working with you!

I am giving you a plant for your classroom because both you and I have done a lot of <u>growing</u> this semester. I've learned so many wonderful things from your teacher and from each one of you! It has been fun learning and sharing together.

You are the very first class of children I have ever taught. I will always hold a special place in my heart for all of you. I loved teaching all of you! You are all very special to me.

Be good and study hard!

Love,

Ms. White

Cooperating Teacher's Completion

As the experience comes to a close, you will have to decide how you would like to culminate the experience. Some cooperating teachers write personal letters to their student teachers that let them know how special they were. Some ideas for completion include the following:

_____ Write a personal message.

_____ Select a small gift that represents teaching (i.e., an apple for the desk, pen/pencil set, a book, etc.).

_____ Make a scrapbook of the experiences you have noticed during the semester, including comments students have made, samples of student work, and photographs with anecdotes and quotes—somewhat like a "Remember When . . . ."

_____ Prepare an audiotaped (or videotaped) message to your student teacher. Instead of writing a letter, use technology to give some reminders about teaching or some helpful hints you haven't had time to say.

_____ Write a poem that expresses your feelings about teaching.

_____ Make a list of helpful hints and frame it for the student teacher's desk—for example, "Develop a philosophy of teaching. Know why you want to be a teacher. Be a life-long learner. Be a professional teacher who relates to the real world outside of the classroom. Know your students and have empathy for their lives. Take risks. Teaching is a process."

_____ Take a photograph of the entire class and frame it.

_____ Compile a photo album to begin the portfolio process for the student teacher (include samples that reflect the student teacher's experiences in your classroom).

Cooperating Teacher's Reflection

How do I feel about completing the experience with my student teacher?

JOURNAL ENTRY

Date: _____

_____

_____

_____

_____

_____

_____

_____

REFLECTIVE QUESTIONS

For the last reflection, use another sheet of paper to answer any of the following questions that stand out for you. Place it in a safe place for future reference.

1. An area of growth and development I noticed in my student teacher

2. Something special that happened with my student teacher during the practicum

3. Something I learned from my student teacher during the practicum

4. Something I learned about myself as a teacher during this experience (How did I grow?)

5. Some worthwhile experiences for me and my classroom

6. Some contributions my student teacher made

7. Things I would do differently next time

8. Would I invite another student teacher into my classroom? Why or why not?

Final Reminders and Helpful Hints

_____ Make sure your student teacher returns any materials borrowed from the school library or from other teachers before leaving

_____ Think about your future relationship with this student teacher. Are you his or her mentor? Will you see this person again? Do you want the student teacher to come back and visit your classroom? When? Completion does not have to mean the relationship is over—in fact, it can be a new beginning! You must set the ground rules for the new relationship.

_____ Encourage your student teacher to write thank you letters to anyone in the building who was of assistance in any way. The college supervisor should also receive a note of thanks.

_____ Use your contacts to assist the student teacher in finding a job if you feel he or she should be hired to teach in the near future.

_____ Acknowledge yourself for being a cooperating teacher this semester!

_____ List your reminders here:

_____

_____

_____

_____

_____

_____

_____

_____

_____

Conclusion

When teachers receive this kind of recognition, they go to extraordinary lengths to justify it. They reflect on their practice, translating intuitive behavior into more conscious, visible information that can be useful to others. This process results in extraordinary learning and classroom improvement for teachers and for students of teaching alike.

Roland S. Barth

The quote above relates to a story Barth shares in his book, *Improving Schools from Within—Teachers, Parents, and Principals Can Make the Difference.* In a chapter titled Between School and University, he recalls the importance of including and recognizing classroom teachers as they participate in their role of teacher educators. The intention of this handbook is to support those cooperating teachers while they are in the process of coaching student teachers. The handbook coaches the cooperating teacher so you are able to translate what you do intuitively.

Recognizing classroom teachers for the role they play as experts of practice and encouraging them to share their ideas in a reflective way enriches any teacher education program. Encouraging reflection, collaboration, discussion, and informal conversation among cooperating teachers and among the student teacher, the cooperating teacher, and the college supervisor is a positive way to enhance the practicum experience.

Chapter 17, which constitutes this final section, invites you to review the practicum experience. As you complete this process with your student teacher, acknowledge yourself for the contribution you have made to the teaching profession. Note the sense of loss or relief you may feel when the student teacher leaves your classroom. What will you do differently or the same as you set goals for future experiences? Keep notes, write in your journal, and continue to share ideas, because each time you articulate your visions for teacher education, we all come one step closer to making teaching a major profession.

CHAPTER 17

Reviewing the Practicum Experience

Remember that your influence begins with you and ripples outward. So be sure that your influence is both potent and wholesome. How do I know that this works? All growth spreads outward from a fertile and potent nucleus. You are a nucleus.

John Heider
The Tao of Leadership

Cooperating teachers are powerful factors in teacher education programs. As a cooperating teacher, your influence ripples out into your student teacher's classroom and on to any cooperating teacher experiences that teacher may have in the future with his or her own student teachers. How you present your knowledge and experiences will influence the profession of teaching. Even in an isolated classroom, a teacher can make a difference by sharing and articulating a vision for teacher education.

This chapter completes this handbook and serves as a final reflection for the whole experience. At the end of the practicum, most cooperating teachers are so busy or so anxious to return to their own teaching routines that reflection is often overlooked, but it should not be. You may also use this as an opportunity to plan for future cooperating teacher experiences. If you are part of a collegial cooperating teacher group, this final chapter can serve as a completion activity for your course or group meetings. Invite your student teacher to review the experience of using the topics suggested in this handbook and share his or her perspective on the experience. The student teacher may want to keep this in a private journal, or you may decide to share your perspectives.

Use the forms in this chapter to complete the experience and review the value of being a cooperating teacher as a professional development activity.

University Supervisor Suggestions

> **PLAN:** **Organize your thoughts and materials, and prepare for your role.**

Key Questions

1. What did I learn from this experience?

2. What will I do differently the next time I supervise?

Teaching Competency Focus Areas for Chapter 17

Knowledge, Communication, Instructional Practice, **Evaluation, Problem Solving**, Equity, & **Professionalism**

> **CONNECT:** **Use resources to enhance your skills as a supervisor.**

People. Who supported you during this experience?

Books and Resources. Which books and resources did you and your student teacher find useful?

Technology. How did you use technology to support your supervision?

> **ACT:** **Select the activities that will be useful to you or create your own.**

ACTion #1. Meet with all the other supervisors and discuss the highs and lows of the semester.

ACTion #2. Meet and discuss supervision with your supervisor.

ACTion #3. Take some time to review the events of the semester by reading your journals.

REFLECT: Think about your role as a supervisor and write a one-page reflection.

Choose to respond to the key questions on the previous page, create a prompt of your own, or answer the following question: What do I notice as an area of professional growth for myself as a supervisor this semester?

Cooperating Teacher's Final Reflection

1. List the three most positive aspects of being a cooperating teacher during this practicum.

   • _____

   • _____

   • _____

2. What would you say to a cooperating teacher who is coaching a student teacher for the first time?

   _____

   _____

3. How do your first impressions of the experience (or of your student teacher) compare to your final thoughts?

   _____

   _____

4. How has this been a professionally rewarding developmental experience for you as a teacher?

   _____

   _____

5. Other thoughts:

   _____

   _____

   _____

Goals for Future Practicum Experiences

If you jotted down ideas throughout the experience on Final Reminders pages or in margins, take the time to review them. Decide which ideas are important to remember as overall goals and list them below. These personal goals should be major issues that would greatly enhance the experience. All cooperating teachers will have different goals.

Example: I will meet with my student teacher two weeks prior to the beginning of the practicum.

Example: I will contact the college supervisor and request a meeting (without the student teacher present) to review any college procedures at the beginning of the practicum.

1. Goal #1

_____

_____

2. Goal #2

_____

_____

3. Goal #3

_____

_____

Other thoughts for the future:

_____

_____

_____